Beyond a reasonable doubt: The case for an afterlife

© 2024 Jamie Stas All rights reserved.

No part of this book may be reproduced, distributed, or transmitted in any form or by any means, including photocopying, recording, or other electronic or mechanical methods, without the prior written permission of the publisher, except in the case of brief quotations embodied in critical reviews and certain other non-commercial uses permitted by copyright law.

For permission requests, please contact the publisher at: info@areghostsreal.info

First Edition: September 2024

Cover Design by: Jamie
Printed in the USA

This is a work of non-fiction. While every effort has been made to ensure the accuracy of the information contained herein, the author and publisher assume no responsibility for errors, omissions, or interpretations of the subject matter.

Introduction 7

Beyond a Reasonable Doubt 9
The Role of Anecdotal Evidence... 11
The Goal of This Exploration.. 13
Exploring the Limitations of Modern Science 14

The Quest for Consciousness.. 16
Introduction: The Enigma of Consciousness 16
The Central Role of Consciousness in Human Existence 17
The Interplay Between Science and Philosophy 19
The Hard Problem of Consciousness...................................... 20
Internal Dialogue.. 22
The Role of Internal Dialogue in Consciousness 23

Theories on consciouness... 26
Introduction.. 26
The Importance of Theorizing Consciousness........................ 26
A Journey Through Competing Theories................................ 27
The Road Ahead 28

The different theories in detail 29
Materialistic theories 29
Global Workspace Theory (GWT) 35
Philosopical theories.. 42
Panpsychism... 47
Orchestrated Objective Reduction.. 54
Integrated theories... 61

Cosmic Entities 71

The Interface Theory of Perception 71

The Intersection of Science and the Unexplained 80

Glimpse into the Unknown 82

Ghosts and Apparitions 87

Types of Ghosts 89

Residual Ghosts 89

The Stone Tape Theory: Recording and Playback 89

Characteristics of Residual Hauntings 91

Implications for the Concept of an Afterlife 93

Intelligent hauntings 95

Characteristics of Intelligent Spirits 95

Theories Behind Intelligent Spirits 98

Poltergeists 101

Theories: Psychokinesis (PK) 102

Conclusion 107

EVP and Advanced Technology 108

The Non-Local Mind: Exploring ESP and Telepathy 116

The Rhine Institute and the Study of ESP 116

Beyond Rhine: Modern Parapsychological Studies 118

The Quantum Brain 120

Mediums 123

Introduction *123*

The Case of Leonora Piper *124*

The Cross-Correspondences *125*

The Rudi Schneider Case *126*

The Case of Chico Xavier *127*

Conclusion *129*

Deathbed and Crisis Apparitions **131**

Case Study: The Ghosts of Flight 401 .... *132*

Other Examples of Deathbed and Crisis Apparitions *134*

Significance of Deathbed and Crisis Apparitions *135*

Reincarnation **137**

Explanation of the Concept of Reincarnation *137*

Irrefutable Cases *142*

The Case of Swarnlata Mishra *142*

The Case of James Leininger: A Detailed Examination *148*

The Case of Shanti Devi: A Detailed Examination **154**

Shanti Devi's Early Memories *154*

The Case of Gopal Gupta: A Detailed Examination *160*

Near Death Experience **168**

Common Elements of NDEs *170*

The stories **173**

The Case of Pam Reynolds *173*

The Case of Maria's Shoe *179*

4

The Case of Dr. Eben Alexander *184*

The common factors in NDE'S *193*

7.3 The Limits of Conventional Theories *194*

Perception Without a Brain *195*

The Implications: A Challenge to Modern Science *196*

Out-of-Body Experiences (OBEs) and Remote Viewing **199**

Remote viewing *199*

Definition and History of Remote Viewing *199*

The CIA's Interest in and Studies on Remote Viewing *199*

The Star Gate Program *200*

Key Findings and Implications *200*

Out-of-Body Experiences *201*

The CIA's Interest in Paranormal Phenomena *212*

Deathbed Visions and Shared Death Experiences **222**

A New Vision of the Afterlife **229**

The Convergence of Evidence **239**

Consciousness and the Quantum Enigma **243**

The Double-Slit Experiment *243*

The Measurement Problem *244*

Delayed-Choice Experiments *245*

The Importance of Consciousness in Shaping Reality *246*

Occam's Razor *247*

Consciousness as the Foundation of Reality **249**

Beyond the Horizon of the Known 250

INTRODUCTION

For centuries, we've been driven by a deep need to understand the world around us. We've built mighty empires, sent ships into the stars, and cracked open the mysteries of the atom. Science has been our most powerful tool, revealing truths about the cosmos and our own existence. Yet, despite all of this, one question remains elusive: What happens after we die? Is there more beyond this life? No matter where you're from or what you believe, this is a question that touches all of us.

This book, *Beyond a Reasonable Doubt: Proof of the Afterlife,* isn't here to prove heaven exists or to declare anything about God. It's not built on religious beliefs or abstract philosophy. Instead, it's a journey—a dive into the evidence suggesting there could be something after this life. We're not here to turn our backs on science but to go beyond its current reach. Science has taken us far, but there are questions it struggles to answer, especially those that step beyond the physical world and the confines of a lab.

In these pages, we'll look closely at phenomena that hint at life beyond death. We'll explore near-death experiences, past-life memories, encounters with apparitions, and strange, unexplainable communications. With an open mind, we'll examine the research, testimonies, and data collected over time. The goal is to see what we can reasonably believe might be true. This isn't about rejecting science. Far from it. It's about acknowledging that science, as we know it, may have its limits. Just as quantum physics reveals mysteries that puzzle even the greatest minds, so too does the study of human consciousness present challenges we can't ignore. At its heart, true science is about pushing boundaries and asking the tough questions.

As you read this book, you might find yourself rethinking things you once believed or confronting ideas that feel new or uncomfortable. That's the essence of exploration. I invite you to walk with me on this journey, to question with an open mind, and to entertain the thought that the afterlife may not just be a matter of faith—it could be something we can reason through and even find evidence for. Together, we'll see what we can discover beyond a reasonable doubt.

BEYOND A REASONABLE DOUBT

The concept of "beyond a reasonable doubt" is one of the most significant standards of proof in the judicial system. It is a standard that requires a level of certainty before reaching a conclusion, especially in criminal cases where the stakes are extraordinarily high. In essence, it means that the evidence presented must be so convincing that there is no reasonable alternative explanation other than the one proposed. It is not about achieving absolute certainty, which is an often-impossible task in complex human affairs, but about reaching a point where the evidence overwhelmingly supports one conclusion over all others. This concept, when applied to the exploration of paranormal phenomena, offers a robust framework for evaluating evidence that exists outside the boundaries of traditional scientific inquiry.

The Legal Standard and Its Relevance to the Paranormal

In a courtroom, proving something "beyond a reasonable doubt" means presenting a case so compelling that the jury feels morally certain of the defendant's guilt. This standard does not require 100% certainty, but it demands a level of assurance that leaves no room for reasonable doubt in the minds of those deliberating the case. When we apply this concept to the exploration of the afterlife and other paranormal phenomena, we are not seeking to prove something with absolute certainty, but rather to assess whether the evidence available is so compelling that it leaves little room for reasonable doubt about the possibility of life beyond death.

Why use a legal standard to explore a metaphysical topic? The answer lies in the nature of the evidence we are dealing with. Unlike traditional scientific research, which relies on repeatable experiments and observable phenomena, much of the evidence for the afterlife comes from personal experiences, historical accounts, and phenomena that are difficult to replicate under controlled conditions. These types of evidence often fall outside the purview of mainstream science, which is predominantly empirical and relies heavily on experimentation and observation. However, just because evidence is anecdotal or non-replicable does not mean it is not worth considering—especially when it accumulates in significant amounts and across diverse contexts.

Beyond a Reasonable Doubt in Science and the Paranormal

Science, in its traditional sense, thrives on the ability to test hypotheses through controlled experiments and measurable results. It relies on a systematic approach to observe, predict, and often, to replicate results. However, there are realms of human experience that are not easily subjected to these methods. The subjective nature of consciousness, the personal experiences of near-death survivors, and the elusive nature of phenomena like apparitions and psychic communications all present challenges to the scientific method. These experiences and phenomena cannot be easily placed under a microscope or recreated in a laboratory setting.

This is where the legal concept of "beyond a reasonable doubt" becomes a useful tool. It allows us to assess the available evidence—not by dismissing it because it does not meet the stringent criteria of scientific proof, but by evaluating whether, given the entirety of the evidence, the most plausible explanation is that there is something beyond our current understanding of life and death. This approach respects the limitations of science while still allowing us to engage with the evidence in a meaningful way.

THE ROLE OF ANECDOTAL EVIDENCE

One of the most significant challenges in exploring the afterlife is the nature of the evidence itself. Many of the accounts of afterlife experiences are deeply personal and anecdotal. These are stories of near-death experiences (NDEs), where individuals report vivid encounters with what they interpret as another realm of existence. There are also accounts of past-life memories, particularly in young children who recall details of lives they seemingly never lived, as well as experiences with apparitions or unexplained communications from deceased loved ones.

In a scientific context, anecdotal evidence is often viewed with skepticism because it is not easily verifiable, replicable, or observable by others. However, in the context of legal reasoning, anecdotal evidence can hold significant weight, especially when it is consistent, credible, and corroborated by multiple independent sources. When we consider a large body of such evidence, patterns begin to emerge, and these patterns can suggest that something genuine is occurring, even if it is not fully understood.

The credibility of witnesses, the consistency of their testimonies, and the lack of alternative explanations all contribute to forming a case that can be considered beyond a reasonable doubt. For instance, when thousands of individuals across different cultures and time periods describe remarkably similar experiences during near-death episodes, it becomes increasingly difficult to dismiss these accounts as mere coincidences or products of imagination.

The Importance of Corroboration and Consistency

In the courtroom, one of the key factors that strengthen a case is the presence of corroborative evidence—different pieces of evidence that, while independent, all point to the same conclusion. This principle is equally valuable when evaluating paranormal phenomena. When different types of evidence—be they NDEs, past-life memories, or verified instances of mediumship—begin to corroborate each other, the case for the afterlife strengthens. Each piece of evidence, when taken alone, might be dismissible, but when viewed collectively, they paint a picture that is hard to ignore.

For example, the phenomenon of children recalling past lives has been documented across various cultures, with many of these children providing details about previous lives that are later verified through historical records. While one such case might be dismissed as coincidence or fabrication, the consistency of these accounts across different cultures and the verifiable details they provide make it challenging to attribute them purely to chance or imagination.

Addressing Skepticism and Alternative Explanations

A fundamental part of proving something beyond a reasonable doubt is addressing alternative explanations. This means considering and ruling out other plausible scenarios that could account for the evidence. In the context of the afterlife, skeptics often propose psychological or neurological explanations for

NDEs, past-life memories, or apparitions. They might argue that these experiences are the result of brain activity during traumatic events, suggestibility, or simply the human mind's propensity to create narratives in the face of the unknown.

While these explanations are worth considering, it is equally important to weigh them against the evidence. For instance, the argument that NDEs are merely hallucinations caused by a dying brain does not fully account for instances where individuals report verifiable information they could not have known—such as events occurring in another room or details of conversations that took place while they were clinically dead. Similarly, neurological explanations for past-life memories do not explain cases where the details provided are so specific and verifiable that they exceed what could be attributed to chance or subconscious memory.

THE GOAL OF THIS EXPLORATION

The purpose of this book is not to provide conclusive proof of the afterlife in the scientific sense, as that would be an impossible task given our current tools and understanding. Instead, the goal is to assess whether, based on the available evidence, it is reasonable to believe in the existence of an afterlife beyond a reasonable doubt. This approach allows us to engage with the evidence on its own terms, without dismissing it simply because it does not fit neatly into the framework of conventional science.

By the end of this book, we aim to present a case that is compelling enough for the reader to consider that, while we may not be able to prove the afterlife with absolute certainty, the evidence available makes it difficult to dismiss the possibility. Like a jury weighing the evidence in a courtroom, we will consider the facts, the testimonies, and the alternative explanations, and we will ask ourselves: Is there enough here to reach a conclusion beyond a reasonable doubt?

As you embark on this journey through the pages that follow, we invite you to keep an open mind and to consider the possibility that the answers to some of life's most profound questions might lie not just in the laboratory, but in the cumulative weight of the evidence that has been gathered from the experiences of countless individuals across time and culture. In doing so, you may find that the case for the afterlife is stronger than you ever imagined.

EXPLORING THE LIMITATIONS OF MODERN SCIENCE

As we venture into the exploration of the afterlife and other paranormal phenomena, it is essential to acknowledge the incredible advancements that modern science has brought to our understanding of the universe. From the intricate workings of the human body to the vast expanses of space, science has provided us with profound insights into the nature of reality. However, as we delve deeper into the mysteries of existence, we begin to encounter the boundaries of what traditional scientific methods can explain. To fully appreciate the complexities of these boundaries, it is necessary to engage in a dialogue with science, examining its strengths, its limitations, and the philosophical concepts that challenge its scope.

The Scope and Limits of Modern Science

Modern science is a powerful tool for exploring and understanding the physical world. It operates on the principles of observation, experimentation, and replication, which have allowed us to develop technologies, cure diseases, and unravel the laws of nature. However, this very methodology, which demands empirical evidence and repeatability, also constrains science to the material aspects of reality—those that can be measured, observed, and tested under controlled conditions.

When it comes to phenomena that are subjective, non-replicable, or transcend the material, science often finds itself at a crossroads. Concepts like consciousness, the afterlife, and paranormal experiences fall into a gray area where traditional scientific tools may not be sufficient. This does not diminish the value of science, but rather highlights the need for a broader approach—one that considers alternative perspectives and philosophical insights to address questions that lie beyond the material world.

THE QUEST FOR CONSCIOUSNESS

INTRODUCTION: THE ENIGMA OF CONSCIOUSNESS

Consciousness stands as one of the most profound and enduring mysteries of human existence. It is the very essence of our experience, the inner voice that narrates our thoughts, emotions, and perceptions. Yet, despite centuries of philosophical debate and scientific inquiry, consciousness remains elusive, defying complete understanding. This chapter delves into the intricate nature of consciousness, exploring why it captivates our curiosity and the central role it plays in both everyday life and the exploration of the paranormal.

Defining Consciousness

At its core, consciousness can be described as the state of being aware of and able to think about one's own existence, sensations, thoughts, and surroundings. It encompasses everything from the simplest awareness of a sound to the complex reflections on life and existence. But defining consciousness goes beyond mere description—it touches the very fabric of what it means to be alive and self-aware.

Consciousness is not just about waking up and interacting with the world; it is the rich tapestry of experiences that make each individual unique. It includes our perceptions, memories, emotions, and the continuous stream of thoughts that shape our understanding of reality. This intricate blend of awareness and cognition makes consciousness a central topic in various fields, including neuroscience, philosophy, psychology, and even the study of paranormal phenomena.

THE CENTRAL ROLE OF CONSCIOUSNESS IN HUMAN EXISTENCE

Consciousness is fundamental to our existence for several reasons:

1. **Self-Identity and Personal Experience**: Consciousness provides us with a sense of self. It allows us to recognize ourselves as distinct entities with our own thoughts, feelings, and experiences. This self-awareness is crucial for personal growth, decision-making, and forming relationships.

2. **Understanding Reality**: Through consciousness, we interpret and make sense of the world around us. Our perceptions are filtered through our conscious mind, shaping our reality based on sensory input and cognitive processes.

3. **Moral and Ethical Frameworks**: Consciousness enables us to contemplate moral and ethical questions. It allows for the development of values, empathy, and the ability to distinguish right from wrong, which are essential for societal cohesion and personal integrity.

4. **Creative and Intellectual Endeavors**: Our conscious mind fuels creativity and intellectual pursuits. It drives innovation, artistic expression, scientific discovery, and philosophical inquiry, pushing the boundaries of what we know and can achieve.

5. **Exploration of the Paranormal**: Consciousness is at the heart of many paranormal phenomena. Experiences such as ghosts, near-death experiences (NDEs), and telepathy challenge our conventional understanding of consciousness, suggesting that it may extend beyond the physical confines of the brain.

Why Consciousness Remains a Mystery

Despite its central role, consciousness remains shrouded in mystery for several reasons:

1. **Subjective Nature**: Consciousness is inherently subjective. It is a first-person experience that is difficult to measure or observe objectively. This subjectivity makes it challenging to study using traditional scientific methods, which rely on external observation and quantifiable data.

2. **The Hard Problem**: Philosopher David Chalmers coined the term "the hard problem of consciousness" to describe the difficulty of explaining how and why subjective experiences arise from physical processes in the brain. While we can map brain activity and understand certain cognitive functions, the leap to subjective experience remains elusive.

3. **Complexity of the Brain**: The human brain is extraordinarily complex, with billions of neurons and trillions of connections. Understanding how these intricate networks give rise to consciousness is a monumental task that continues to baffle scientists and philosophers alike.

4. **Interdisciplinary Challenges**: Consciousness spans multiple disciplines, including neuroscience, psychology, philosophy, and even quantum physics. Integrating insights from these diverse fields to form a cohesive understanding of consciousness is a significant challenge.

5. **Philosophical Debates**: There are numerous philosophical perspectives on consciousness, each

offering different explanations and frameworks. From dualism, which separates mind and body, to materialism, which views consciousness as a byproduct of physical processes, these debates add layers of complexity to our quest for understanding.

THE INTERPLAY BETWEEN SCIENCE AND PHILOSOPHY

The quest to understand consciousness is a dance between science and philosophy, each offering unique insights and approaches:

1. **Scientific Approaches**: Neuroscience seeks to unravel the neural correlates of consciousness, mapping brain activity to conscious experiences. Cognitive psychology explores how mental processes influence behavior and perception. Quantum physics even ventures into the role of consciousness in the fabric of reality itself.

2. **Philosophical Perspectives**: Philosophy grapples with the nature of consciousness, questioning its origins, existence, and implications. Concepts like dualism, panpsychism, and idealism provide frameworks for understanding consciousness beyond the materialistic view.

3. **Integrative Theories**: Some theories attempt to bridge the gap between science and philosophy. For example, Integrated Information Theory (IIT) proposes that consciousness arises from the integration of information within a system, blending scientific principles with philosophical inquiry.

4. **Pop Culture Influence**: Science fiction and popular media often explore themes of consciousness, presenting imaginative scenarios that inspire both scientific research and philosophical debate. Stories like "The Matrix" and

"Inception" challenge our perceptions of reality and consciousness, reflecting and shaping public discourse.

THE HARD PROBLEM OF CONSCIOUSNESS

At the heart of the enigma lies the hard problem: why and how does consciousness arise from physical processes? While we can observe brain activity and correlate it with certain experiences, the subjective quality of consciousness—the "what it feels like" aspect—remains unexplained.

1. **Explanatory Gap**: There is a significant gap between understanding the mechanisms of the brain and explaining subjective experiences. This gap highlights the limitations of a purely materialistic approach and suggests that consciousness may involve elements beyond the physical.

2. **Implications for Understanding Reality**: Solving the hard problem could revolutionize our understanding of reality, bridging the gap between the physical and the experiential. It could provide insights into the nature of existence, the possibility of life after death, and the true potential of the human mind.

3. **Challenging Materialism**: The hard problem challenges the materialistic view that consciousness is merely a byproduct of brain activity. It opens the door to alternative theories that view consciousness as fundamental, pervasive, and possibly eternal.

Embracing the Mystery

Consciousness remains one of the most profound and captivating mysteries of human existence. Its central role in shaping our identity, understanding of reality, and exploration of the paranormal underscores its significance. As we journey through this book, the enigma of consciousness will serve as a guiding star, illuminating the path as we delve into the mysteries of the afterlife, paranormal phenomena, and the very essence of what it means to be conscious.

By embracing the mystery of consciousness and remaining open to diverse theories and experiences, we position ourselves to uncover deeper truths about life, death, and the possibilities that lie beyond our current understanding. The quest to understand consciousness is not just an academic pursuit; it is a journey into the heart of existence itself, inviting us to explore the unknown with curiosity, wonder, and an unwavering commitment to uncovering the truth.

INTERNAL DIALOGUE

THE INNER VOICE

One of the most immediate and relatable aspects of consciousness is the phenomenon of internal dialogue, also known as "the inner voice" or "self-talk." This is the ongoing conversation we have with ourselves throughout our waking hours, a stream of thoughts that reflects our emotions, plans, fears, and desires. Far from being a trivial byproduct of mental activity, internal dialogue plays a crucial role in our understanding of consciousness, self-identity, and the nature of subjective experience.

Defining Internal Dialogue

Internal dialogue refers to the verbalized thoughts we experience internally, often in the form of self-reflective questions, affirmations, doubts, and observations. It is an integral part of our mental life, influencing how we process information, make decisions, and relate to the world around us.

This inner conversation is more than just a sequence of thoughts; it represents a complex cognitive process where the mind engages in self-reflection, considers alternatives, and navigates the intricacies of daily life. The internal dialogue is not limited to language alone; it often includes imagery, emotions, and even bodily sensations that contribute to the overall experience.

THE ROLE OF INTERNAL DIALOGUE IN CONSCIOUSNESS

1. **Self-Awareness and Identity**: Internal dialogue is central to the development of self-awareness. It allows individuals to reflect on their thoughts, emotions, and experiences, fostering a sense of identity. Through self-talk, we can analyze our behaviors, set personal goals, and evaluate our actions, all of which contribute to a coherent sense of self.

2. **Decision-Making and Problem-Solving**: The internal dialogue is instrumental in decision-making and problem-solving. By engaging in a mental dialogue, we weigh pros and cons, consider various outcomes, and arrive at decisions. This process often involves reasoning through different scenarios and anticipating potential consequences, demonstrating the cognitive complexity inherent in consciousness.

3. **Emotional Regulation**: Internal dialogue plays a key role in regulating emotions. It allows individuals to process and make sense of their feelings, offering a means to manage stress, anxiety, and other emotional states. Positive self-talk, for example, can bolster confidence and resilience, while negative self-talk might contribute to self-doubt and anxiety.

4. **Moral and Ethical Reflection**: The inner voice is also where we grapple with moral and ethical dilemmas. It is through this internal conversation that we reflect on right and wrong, consider the impact of our actions on others, and align our behaviors with our values and principles. This reflective process is essential for developing a moral compass and navigating complex social interactions.

5. **Creativity and Imagination**: Internal dialogue fuels creativity and imagination. It is in these mental spaces that we explore new ideas, solve creative problems, and engage in imaginative thinking. The internal dialogue often serves as a brainstorming session where thoughts and ideas are freely exchanged, leading to innovative solutions and artistic expression.

IMPLICATIONS OF INTERNAL DIALOGUE

The Continuity of Consciousness: Internal dialogue suggests that consciousness is a continuous and dynamic process. Even when not engaged in external activities, the mind remains active, reflecting an ongoing stream of consciousness that contributes to our understanding of time, memory, and personal continuity.

1. **Subjectivity and the First-Person Perspective**: The internal dialogue underscores the deeply subjective nature of consciousness. Each person's inner voice is unique, shaped by their individual experiences, beliefs, and emotions. This subjectivity highlights the challenge of studying consciousness objectively, as much of what we know about the mind is experienced from a first-person perspective.

2. **The Mind's Capacity for Self-Reflection**: The presence of internal dialogue illustrates the mind's remarkable ability to reflect upon itself. This meta-cognitive capacity—thinking about thinking—is a hallmark of human consciousness and suggests that consciousness is not just a passive state but an active, self-aware process.

3. **Challenges to Materialism**: The complexity and richness of internal dialogue challenge strictly materialistic views of consciousness. If consciousness were merely a byproduct of neural processes, how do we account for

the depth, creativity, and ethical reasoning that internal dialogue encompasses? This question opens the door to alternative theories of consciousness that consider it as more than just a brain function.

4. **Potential Insights into Paranormal Phenomena**: Internal dialogue might also offer insights into paranormal phenomena. For example, experiences such as mediumship, where individuals claim to communicate with spirits, could be seen as an extension or alteration of internal dialogue. Similarly, during near-death experiences (NDEs), individuals often report heightened or transformed internal dialogues, suggesting that consciousness, and by extension internal dialogue, might persist beyond the physical body.

INTERNAL DIALOGUE IN THE CONTEXT OF THE HARD PROBLEM

The internal dialogue provides a tangible example of the "hard problem" of consciousness—how and why subjective experiences arise from physical processes in the brain. While we can study brain activity associated with internal dialogue, the subjective experience itself, the "what it feels like" to engage in self-talk, remains elusive. This underscores the gap between objective observation and subjective experience, making internal dialogue a crucial area of focus in the quest to understand consciousness.

THEORIES ON CONSCIOUNESS

INTRODUCTION

This chapter serves as an introduction to the diverse and sometimes competing theories of consciousness that have been proposed over the years. From the materialistic frameworks that dominate contemporary science to the more esoteric and philosophical models, each theory offers a different lens through which to view the enigma of consciousness. These theories not only seek to explain how consciousness arises but also explore what it means for our understanding of reality, self-awareness, and even the possibility of life beyond the physical realm.

THE IMPORTANCE OF THEORIZING CONSCIOUSNESS

Understanding consciousness is not just an academic exercise; it has profound implications for nearly every aspect of human experience. Our theories of consciousness shape how we perceive ourselves, our interactions with others, and our understanding of the world around us. They inform our approaches to mental health, ethics, artificial intelligence, and the very nature of reality itself.

Moreover, consciousness is central to many of the paranormal phenomena explored in this book—whether it's the persistence of consciousness after death, as suggested by ghost sightings and near-death experiences, or the idea that consciousness might extend beyond the individual mind in cases of telepathy and reincarnation. By examining the theories of consciousness, we can begin to understand how such phenomena might be possible and what they reveal about the true nature of consciousness.

A JOURNEY THROUGH COMPETING THEORIES

This chapter will take you on a journey through the most influential theories of consciousness, starting with the materialistic views that dominate contemporary neuroscience and psychology. We will explore:

- **Materialistic Theories**: These theories, grounded in physicalism, argue that consciousness arises from the brain's physical processes. We will delve into the Neural Correlates of Consciousness (NCCs), computational models, and other scientific approaches that seek to explain consciousness as a product of brain activity.
- **Philosophical Perspectives**: Moving beyond strict materialism, we will consider philosophical theories that challenge the reductionist view of consciousness. This includes dualism, which separates mind and body; panpsychism, which suggests that consciousness is a fundamental property of all matter; and idealism, which posits that consciousness is the primary substance of reality.
- **Integrative and Esoteric Models**: Finally, we will explore integrative theories like Integrated Information Theory (IIT), which combines aspects of materialism with a broader understanding of information and consciousness, and esoteric models that propose consciousness as a universal or cosmic phenomenon.

Each of these theories offers a different way of understanding the mind and its relationship to the world, highlighting the complexity and richness of the study of consciousness.

THE ROAD AHEAD

As we delve into these theories, it's important to approach them with an open mind. The nature of consciousness is a topic that transcends easy explanations, and each theory brings us closer to understanding the full picture, even if no single theory can yet claim to provide all the answers.

By exploring the various theories of consciousness, we aim to build a foundation for the rest of this book. As we investigate paranormal phenomena, the insights gained from these theories will help us make sense of experiences that challenge conventional understanding and open the door to new ways of thinking about life, death, and the nature of reality itself.

In the chapters that follow, we will unpack these theories in greater detail, examining their strengths, limitations, and implications for the mysteries that lie at the heart of human existence.

THE DIFFERENT THEORIES IN DETAIL

MATERIALISTIC THEORIES

MATERIALISM AND CONSCIOUSNESS

Materialism stands as one of the most influential and widely accepted frameworks in the study of consciousness. It is grounded in the belief that everything in the universe, including consciousness, can be understood through physical processes and matter. This perspective has shaped much of contemporary science, especially in fields like neuroscience, psychology, and cognitive science. In this chapter, we will explore the core principles of materialism, its applications in explaining consciousness, and examine both its strengths and limitations, particularly concerning paranormal phenomena.

Core Concepts of Materialism

At the core of materialism lies the idea that all phenomena, including consciousness, arise from physical processes. Within this framework, the mind is not seen as separate from the body; instead, it is entirely dependent on the brain's physical operations. Mental states such as thoughts, emotions, and subjective experiences are viewed as byproducts of neural activity—complex interactions of electrical and chemical signals within the brain.

- **Brain as a Machine**: Materialism often likens the brain to an intricate machine or computer. Just as a computer processes data via hardware and software, the brain processes information through neurons and synapses,

generating consciousness as an emergent result of these operations.
- **Reductionism**: A central aspect of materialism is reductionism—the belief that complex phenomena can be understood by breaking them down into simpler components. In terms of consciousness, this implies that mental states are reducible to physical states, such as neuronal firing or neurotransmitter release.

Neural Correlates of Consciousness (NCCs)

One of the key objectives of materialistic approaches is to identify the Neural Correlates of Consciousness (NCCs)—the specific brain structures and activities corresponding to conscious experiences. By mapping these correlates, researchers aim to pinpoint the brain regions responsible for various aspects of consciousness, such as perception, thought, and emotion.

- **Brain Imaging Techniques**: Technologies such as fMRI and EEG allow researchers to observe brain activity in real-time, helping identify which areas of the brain are active during different conscious states.
- **Localization of Function**: Materialism often emphasizes the localization of function, where different brain regions are associated with specific cognitive processes. For example, the visual cortex is responsible for processing visual input, while the prefrontal cortex is crucial for decision-making and self-reflection.

Consciousness as an Emergent Property

Materialism views consciousness as an emergent property—arising from the intricate interactions of simpler elements within the brain, such as neurons and synapses. This suggests that while consciousness is more than just the sum of its parts, it cannot exist without the underlying physical processes.

- **Complex Systems**: Consciousness is seen as a product of complex systems, much like other emergent phenomena such as life or weather, arising from the interplay of simpler components.
- **Continuum of Consciousness**: Materialism supports the idea that consciousness exists on a continuum, with varying levels of complexity depending on the brain's structure and function, ranging from simple organisms with basic awareness to humans with advanced self-consciousness.

Advantages of Materialism in Explaining Consciousness

Materialism is rooted in empirical evidence, relying on observable and measurable phenomena. This approach enables the systematic study of consciousness through experiments, brain imaging, and other scientific methods. The ability to gather and analyze data makes materialism a powerful framework for understanding the brain's role in generating consciousness.

Clear and Testable Predictions

Materialist theories offer clear, testable predictions about how consciousness operates. For example, materialism predicts that damage to certain brain regions will result in specific deficits, such as memory loss or personality changes. These predictions can be validated through clinical research, making materialism a valuable approach in diagnosing and treating neurological conditions.

Integration with Other Scientific Disciplines

Materialism harmonizes with other scientific disciplines, including biology, chemistry, and physics. By treating consciousness as a physical phenomenon, it encourages interdisciplinary research, leading to advancements in fields like neuropharmacology, where the chemical foundations of consciousness are explored.

Technological Applications

The materialist perspective has led to practical applications in medicine and technology. For instance, brain-computer interfaces (BCIs) and neuroprosthetics have been developed based on the understanding that electrical brain activity can be harnessed to control devices or restore functions, significantly improving the quality of life for people with disabilities.

Limitations of Materialism in Explaining Consciousness

The Hard Problem of Consciousness

A significant challenge for materialism is the "hard problem" of consciousness, introduced by philosopher David Chalmers. It refers to the difficulty in explaining how and why physical processes in the brain lead to subjective experiences—the inner sense of what it feels like to be conscious. While materialism can explain brain mechanisms, it struggles to account for the qualitative nature of conscious experience.

The Explanatory Gap

Materialism faces what is often called the "explanatory gap" between physical brain processes and subjective experience. For instance, while materialism can map the neural activity involved in perceiving the color red, it cannot fully explain why that specific neural activity produces the experience of "redness." This gap suggests that materialism may be limited in fully explaining consciousness.

Neglect of Subjective Experience

Critics argue that materialism tends to overlook the richness of subjective experience by focusing too much on objective, measurable phenomena. This reductionist view may miss key aspects of consciousness, such as emotions, thoughts, and the sense of self, which are not easily reducible to physical brain states.

Limited Scope for Paranormal Phenomena

Materialism also struggles to account for certain paranormal phenomena that suggest consciousness might extend beyond the physical brain. Experiences like near-death experiences (NDEs), telepathy, or reincarnation challenge the materialist view, which posits that consciousness is entirely dependent on brain activity.

Materialism and Paranormal Phenomena

Materialism often clashes with accounts of paranormal phenomena that imply consciousness could exist or function independently of the brain. Here's how materialism typically addresses some key paranormal experiences:

- **Near-Death Experiences (NDEs)**: Materialism usually explains NDEs as hallucinations caused by brain activity during stress or lack of oxygen, though this does not explain cases where verifiable experiences occur during periods of minimal brain activity.
- **Telepathy and ESP**: Materialism dismisses telepathy and ESP as coincidental or a result of cognitive biases, lacking a known physical mechanism for transferring information between minds.
- **Reincarnation and Past-Life Memories**: Cases of reincarnation, where individuals recall detailed information about past lives, are difficult for materialism to explain and are often attributed to false memories or cryptomnesia.

Conclusion

While materialism remains a dominant framework in the study of consciousness, offering a scientifically grounded approach that has led to advances in neuroscience, it faces challenges, especially in addressing subjective experience and paranormal phenomena. Understanding both its strengths and limitations is key to advancing the field of consciousness research.

https://journals.sagepub.com/doi/10.1177/02632764211012047

GLOBAL WORKSPACE THEORY (GWT)

Introduction

Global Workspace Theory (GWT) is one of the most influential models in the study of consciousness. First introduced by cognitive scientist Bernard Baars in the 1980s, GWT provides a framework for understanding how consciousness emerges from brain activity. The theory suggests that consciousness arises when information becomes widely accessible to different parts of the brain, allowing this information to be integrated and shared across various cognitive systems.

In this chapter, we will explore the fundamental principles of GWT, focusing on how widespread access to information in the brain leads to consciousness. Particular emphasis will be placed on the roles of the frontal and parietal regions. Additionally, we will discuss the strengths and limitations of GWT, especially in relation to explaining consciousness and its relevance to paranormal phenomena.

Core Concepts of Global Workspace Theory

At the heart of GWT is the idea that consciousness functions as a "global workspace" in the brain—a metaphorical stage where different types of information are brought together and made accessible to multiple cognitive systems. According to this theory, most brain processes operate unconsciously and in parallel. However, when information needs to be integrated, it is "broadcast" to the global workspace, becoming conscious and accessible to systems like memory, decision-making, and motor control.

This broad availability of information is what distinguishes conscious from unconscious processes. For instance, while reading a book, the words you consciously perceive are available not only to your visual system but also to those involved in language comprehension, memory, and emotions. This integration allows for flexible and cohesive responses to complex situations, a defining feature of conscious experience.

The Role of the Frontal and Parietal Regions

GWT places special importance on the frontal and parietal regions of the brain, which are key to maintaining and broadcasting information within the global workspace. These regions are central to higher cognitive functions, such as attention, decision-making, and working memory, all of which are critical to consciousness.

- **Frontal Cortex**: The frontal cortex is responsible for executive functions, including planning, decision-making, and problem-solving. GWT suggests that this region plays a major role in managing the global workspace by directing attention to relevant information and coordinating its integration across different cognitive systems.
- **Parietal Cortex**: The parietal cortex, especially the posterior parietal cortex, is involved in sensory integration and spatial awareness. Within GWT, the parietal cortex helps bring sensory information into the global workspace, contributing to the construction of a unified and coherent conscious experience.

These regions work in tandem to create a dynamic system that allows the brain to prioritize, integrate, and make information available for conscious thought and action.

Advantages of Global Workspace Theory in Explaining Consciousness

Comprehensive Integration of Information

One of the key strengths of GWT is its ability to explain how diverse pieces of information are combined into a unified conscious experience. By proposing that consciousness emerges from the global availability of information, GWT accounts for the seamless nature of conscious experience—how we perceive, think, and act in an integrated and meaningful manner.

Alignment with Neuroscientific Evidence

GWT is supported by substantial neuroscientific evidence. Brain imaging studies, such as those using fMRI, have shown that conscious awareness is linked to widespread brain activity, particularly in the frontal and parietal regions. These findings are consistent with GWT's idea that consciousness involves the global broadcasting of information across the brain.

Flexibility and Adaptability

The theory also explains the flexibility and adaptability of conscious thought. Because information in the global workspace is accessible to multiple cognitive systems, consciousness allows for creative problem-solving, decision-making, and the ability to adapt to new situations. This adaptability is a major evolutionary advantage and helps explain why consciousness is such a central feature of human cognition.

Practical Applications

GWT has practical applications, particularly in understanding and addressing neurological and psychological conditions. For example, the theory has been used to explain disorders of consciousness, such as coma and vegetative states, where the global workspace may be impaired. It also offers insights into conditions like schizophrenia, where disruptions in the global workspace may lead to disorganized thinking and perception.

Limitations of Global Workspace Theory in Explaining Consciousness

The Hard Problem of Consciousness

Like many materialistic theories, GWT struggles with the "hard problem" of consciousness—the challenge of explaining why certain brain processes are accompanied by subjective experience. While GWT can describe how information is integrated and broadcast in the brain, it does not fully explain why this results in the feeling of being conscious or having subjective experiences.

Lack of Specificity

Some critics argue that GWT lacks detail in describing how the global workspace functions. While the theory suggests that information becomes conscious when it is globally accessible, it does not specify how this transition occurs or why certain types of information enter the global workspace while others remain unconscious.

Limited Scope for Explaining Paranormal Phenomena

As a theory rooted in cognitive neuroscience, GWT may be limited in its ability to explain paranormal phenomena, such as near-death experiences (NDEs), telepathy, or mediumship. These phenomena suggest that consciousness might extend beyond the physical brain, challenging the idea that it is solely a product of brain activity.

Overemphasis on the Frontal and Parietal Regions

Although GWT focuses on the frontal and parietal regions, some researchers argue that consciousness cannot be fully explained by focusing on these areas alone. Other regions, such as the thalamus and brainstem, are also crucial in maintaining consciousness, suggesting that a more comprehensive approach may be needed to account for the complexity of conscious experience.

Global Workspace Theory and Paranormal Phenomena

While GWT provides a robust framework for understanding how consciousness emerges from brain processes, its application to paranormal phenomena presents challenges. Although GWT excels at explaining how the brain integrates and accesses information, it does not readily account for experiences that seem to extend beyond the physical brain.

- **Near-Death Experiences (NDEs)**: NDEs often involve vivid conscious experiences during periods of minimal or no brain activity, such as during cardiac arrest. GWT would struggle to explain these experiences, as it relies on active brain processes to generate consciousness.
- **Telepathy and Extrasensory Perception (ESP)**: Phenomena like telepathy suggest that consciousness could extend beyond individual brains, enabling communication between minds. GWT's focus on the brain's internal processes does not account for such inter-brain interactions.
- **Mediumship and Spirit Communication**: Cases of mediumship, where individuals claim to communicate

with spirits, also challenge GWT, as these experiences imply that consciousness might exist independently of the brain, contradicting the materialistic assumptions of the theory.

Conclusion

Global Workspace Theory offers a compelling model for understanding how consciousness arises from brain activity, particularly through the integration and broadcasting of information across various brain regions. Its emphasis on the frontal and parietal regions aligns with neuroscientific evidence, and the theory provides valuable insights into the adaptive nature of conscious thought.

However, GWT faces challenges in addressing the hard problem of consciousness and explaining paranormal phenomena that suggest consciousness may extend beyond the physical brain. While GWT remains an important theory in the study of consciousness, it may need to be revised or supplemented to offer a more comprehensive understanding.

PHILOSOPHICAL THEORIES

DUALISM AND CONSCIOUSNESS

Introduction

Dualism is one of the oldest and most enduring theories of consciousness, with roots in ancient philosophy and a resurgence in prominence through René Descartes in the 17th century. At its core, dualism posits that the mind and body are distinct entities, fundamentally different in nature. While the body is physical and operates according to the laws of physics, the mind—or consciousness—is seen as non-physical and cannot be fully explained by material processes.

This chapter explores the key concepts of dualism, its various forms, and the implications of separating mind and body for our understanding of consciousness. We will also examine the strengths and limitations of dualism, especially its relevance to paranormal phenomena.

Core Concepts of Dualism

The Separation of Mind and Body

Dualism asserts that the mind and body are two separate realms of existence, a perspective often called "substance dualism." This idea suggests that the mind, or soul, is a non-physical substance that exists independently of the physical body.

- **Mind as Non-Physical**: The mind is characterized by thoughts, emotions, intentions, and self-awareness. It is

viewed as immaterial and distinct from the physical world, making it difficult to measure or observe directly.
- **Body as Physical**: The body, including the brain, belongs to the physical world and operates according to biological and chemical processes, governed by the same natural laws that apply to all matter, such as gravity and motion.

Interactionism: How Mind and Body Communicate

A central question in dualism is how the mind and body interact if they are separate entities. Descartes proposed "interactionism," which suggests that, despite their differences, the mind and body communicate with each other.

- **The Pineal Gland**: Descartes believed the pineal gland, a small structure in the brain, served as the point of interaction between the non-physical mind and the physical body. Although modern science has dismissed this specific claim, the question of how these two realms interact remains central to dualist thinking.
- **Mind-Body Causation**: Interactionism holds that mental states can influence physical actions and vice versa. For instance, the desire to move (a mental state) can cause the physical action of movement, while physical experiences like touching a hot surface can generate the mental experience of pain.

Advantages of Dualism in Explaining Consciousness

Addressing the Hard Problem of Consciousness

One of dualism's greatest strengths is its ability to address the "hard problem" of consciousness—the challenge of explaining how subjective experiences arise from physical processes. Dualism sidesteps this by positing that consciousness is non-physical, and therefore does not need to explain how material substances produce subjective experience.

Intuitive Appeal

Dualism aligns with many people's intuitive sense that the mind is distinct from the body. Moments of introspection, emotional reflection, or altered states of consciousness often reinforce the feeling that mental phenomena are not easily reduced to physical processes, supporting the dualist view.

Flexibility in Explaining Paranormal Phenomena

Dualism also provides a framework for understanding paranormal phenomena that imply the mind can exist separately from the body:

- **Near-Death Experiences (NDEs)**: Dualism suggests that during NDEs, the mind or soul temporarily leaves the physical body before returning when the body revives.
- **Mediumship and Spirit Communication**: Dualism supports the notion that consciousness persists after death, allowing for possible communication between spirits and the living.

- **Out-of-Body Experiences (OBEs)**: Dualism naturally accounts for OBEs, where individuals report observing the world from a perspective outside their physical body.

Limitations of Dualism in Explaining Consciousness

The Interaction Problem

A major challenge for dualism is explaining how a non-physical mind can interact with a physical body. If the mind exists in a separate realm, how does it influence or respond to physical events? Despite centuries of debate, dualism has yet to offer a satisfying answer to this "interaction problem."

Lack of Empirical Evidence

Substance dualism lacks empirical support. Neuroscience consistently finds correlations between brain activity and mental states, suggesting that consciousness is closely tied to physical processes. This evidence challenges dualism's claim that the mind exists independently of the body.

Occam's Razor

Critics argue that dualism violates Occam's Razor—the principle that the simplest explanation is usually the correct one. By introducing a separate, non-physical realm to explain consciousness, dualism complicates the picture without necessarily offering greater explanatory power. Materialism, which attributes consciousness to physical processes, offers a more streamlined and parsimonious explanation.

Conclusion

Dualism remains a significant and influential theory in the study of consciousness, offering a distinct perspective that separates the mind and body as fundamentally different entities. Its ability to address the hard problem of consciousness and its alignment with common intuitions about the mind make it an appealing framework, especially for those interested in non-physical aspects of consciousness.

However, dualism faces significant challenges, particularly in explaining how the mind and body interact and in the lack of empirical evidence for a non-physical mind. These issues, along with the theory's complexities, have led many in the scientific community to favor materialistic explanations. Despite these challenges, dualism continues to be a valuable framework for exploring paranormal phenomena and remains an important counterpoint to materialism in the ongoing study of consciousness.

https://en.wikipedia.org/wiki/Mind%E2%80%93body_dualism

PANPSYCHISM

Introduction

Panpsychism is a philosophical theory that has gained renewed interest in recent years as an alternative to both materialism and dualism in the study of consciousness. This theory proposes that consciousness is a fundamental property of all matter, not just of complex organisms like humans. According to panpsychism, even the simplest particles—such as electrons or quarks—possess some form of consciousness, albeit in a very basic or primitive form.

This chapter explores the core concepts of panpsychism, its implications for our understanding of consciousness, and its strengths and limitations, particularly in relation to the scientific study of consciousness and its potential to explain paranormal phenomena.

THE CORE CONCEPTS OF PANPSYCHISM

Consciousness as a Fundamental Property

At the heart of panpsychism is the idea that consciousness is not an emergent property of complex brain processes, as materialism suggests, but a fundamental aspect of reality. This means that consciousness is as basic as other physical properties, such as mass, charge, or spin.

- **Ubiquity of Consciousness**: In panpsychism, consciousness is everywhere and in everything. Every particle in the universe, no matter how small or simple,

has some degree of consciousness. This does not mean that atoms or rocks have thoughts or emotions like humans do, but rather that they possess a rudimentary form of experience or awareness.
- **Non-Emergent Consciousness**: Unlike emergent theories, which argue that consciousness arises from the complexity of neural networks in the brain, panpsychism suggests that consciousness does not "emerge" but is already present in all matter. Complex forms of consciousness, like human self-awareness, are seen as aggregations of simpler forms of consciousness present in the brain's constituent particles.

The Combination Problem

One of the central challenges for panpsychism is known as the "combination problem." This problem concerns how simple forms of consciousness at the level of individual particles combine to form the rich, unified consciousness experienced by complex organisms like humans.

- **Micro-consciousnesses**: If every particle has its own form of consciousness, how do these individual micro-consciousnesses combine to create the unified experience of human consciousness? This question remains a significant theoretical challenge for panpsychism, as it is not clear how individual conscious experiences could combine to form a coherent whole.
- **Proposed Solutions**: Some proponents of panpsychism suggest that just as particles combine to form more complex physical structures, their associated forms of consciousness might also combine to form more complex

mental states. However, this remains an area of active debate and research within the panpsychist framework.

Variations of Panpsychism

Panpsychism is not a monolithic theory; it has several variations that offer different perspectives on how consciousness is distributed throughout the universe:

- **Constitutive Panpsychism**: This form of panpsychism holds that consciousness at the macro level (such as in humans) is constituted by the consciousness of micro-level entities (such as particles or neurons). In this view, human consciousness is nothing more than the sum of its parts.
- **Russellian Monism**: Named after the philosopher Bertrand Russell, this variation posits that consciousness is the intrinsic nature of physical matter. In this view, what we perceive as physical properties are merely the outward appearances of underlying conscious experiences.
- **Cosmopsychism**: A more holistic version of panpsychism, cosmopsychism suggests that the entire universe has a form of consciousness, with individual minds being fragments of this universal mind. This view aligns somewhat with ancient and spiritual notions of a cosmic or universal consciousness.

PROS OF PANPSYCHISM IN EXPLAINING CONSCIOUSNESS

Panpsychism offers several strengths that make it an attractive theory for understanding consciousness:

Addressing the Hard Problem of Consciousness

Panpsychism provides a unique approach to the hard problem of consciousness by eliminating the need to explain how consciousness arises from non-conscious matter. If consciousness is a fundamental property of all matter, then the question of how consciousness comes into existence is bypassed—consciousness is simply a given aspect of the universe.

Avoidance of Dualism's Interaction Problem

By proposing that consciousness is a property of all matter, panpsychism avoids the interaction problem that plagues dualism. Since consciousness and matter are not separate substances but two aspects of the same thing, there is no need to explain how they interact—consciousness is already inherent in the physical world.

Intuitive Appeal and Holistic Perspective

Panpsychism aligns with certain intuitive and holistic perspectives on consciousness, such as the idea that the universe is interconnected and that all things are, in some sense, "alive" or aware. This perspective resonates with many philosophical, spiritual, and indigenous worldviews that see consciousness as a pervasive, fundamental aspect of reality.

Relevance to Quantum Physics

Some interpretations of quantum physics suggest that consciousness may play a role in the behavior of particles at the quantum level. Panpsychism offers a framework that could potentially integrate consciousness into the fabric of quantum mechanics, although this remains speculative and controversial.

CONS OF PANPSYCHISM IN EXPLAINING CONSCIOUSNESS

Despite its strengths, panpsychism faces several significant challenges and criticisms:

The Combination Problem

The combination problem remains one of the most serious challenges for panpsychism. How do simple, individual conscious experiences combine to form the rich, unified consciousness of complex organisms? This question has yet to be satisfactorily answered, making it difficult to see how panpsychism can fully account for human consciousness.

Lack of Empirical Evidence

Like dualism, panpsychism struggles with a lack of empirical evidence. While it is a coherent philosophical theory, there is no direct scientific evidence to support the idea that basic particles possess consciousness. The theory remains largely speculative and philosophical, with few concrete ways to test or measure the consciousness of particles.

Vagueness and Ambiguity

Panpsychism can be criticized for being too vague or ambiguous. What does it mean for a particle to have "consciousness"? How can we define or measure such a form of consciousness? The lack of clear definitions and criteria makes panpsychism difficult to work with in scientific contexts, where precise measurements and clear concepts are crucial.

Panpsychism challenges many established scientific paradigms, particularly the materialist view that consciousness arises from complex brain processes. Integrating panpsychism with existing scientific frameworks would require a significant shift in how we understand both consciousness and matter, a shift that many scientists are hesitant to make without more concrete evidence.

Panpsychism offers intriguing possibilities for explaining certain paranormal phenomena, particularly those that suggest consciousness is more pervasive or fundamental than traditionally believed:

The idea that consciousness is a fundamental property of all matter could potentially explain telepathy or other forms of extrasensory perception (ESP). If consciousness is universal, then it might be possible for minds to connect or communicate across distances, bypassing the need for physical interaction.

Reincarnation and Past-Life Memories

Panpsychism might also offer a framework for understanding reincarnation or past-life memories. If consciousness is not confined to individual brains but is a fundamental aspect of the universe, then it might persist or re-emerge in different forms, aligning with the idea of reincarnation.

Conclusion: The Role of Panpsychism in Consciousness Research

Panpsychism offers a bold and unconventional approach to the study of consciousness, proposing that consciousness is a fundamental property of all matter, from the simplest particles to the most complex organisms. This theory addresses some of the major challenges faced by materialism and dualism, particularly the hard problem of consciousness and the interaction problem.

However, panpsychism also faces significant challenges, including the combination problem and the lack of empirical evidence. While it provides a thought-provoking alternative to more traditional theories.

Nevertheless, panpsychism's potential to explain certain paranormal phenomena and its alignment with holistic and spiritual perspectives make it a valuable and intriguing theory. As we continue to explore different theories of consciousness, panpsychism invites us to consider the possibility that consciousness is not just a product of complex brains but a fundamental aspect of the universe itself.

https://en.wikipedia.org/wiki/Panpsychism

https://www.academia.edu/7754047/Alles_is_bezield_de_opko mst_van_het_panpsychisme

ORCHESTRATED OBJECTIVE REDUCTION

Introduction

Orchestrated Objective Reduction (Orch-OR) is a theory of consciousness that seeks to connect the fields of neuroscience and quantum physics. Developed by physicist Sir Roger Penrose and anesthesiologist Stuart Hameroff, Orch-OR posits that consciousness emerges from quantum processes within the brain's microtubules, tiny structures inside neurons. This theory diverges from traditional materialistic approaches by introducing quantum mechanics as a fundamental element of consciousness.

In this chapter, we will explore the core principles of Orch-OR, its implications for understanding consciousness, and its strengths and limitations. We will also examine how the scientific community has received this theory and its potential to explain paranormal phenomena.

Core Concepts of Orchestrated Objective Reduction

Quantum Mechanics and Consciousness

Orch-OR is based on principles of quantum mechanics, a branch of physics that describes the behavior of particles at the smallest scales. Quantum mechanics is known for its perplexing phenomena, such as superposition (where particles exist in multiple states simultaneously) and entanglement (where particles are instantaneously connected across distances). Penrose and Hameroff suggest that these quantum effects could play a key role in generating consciousness.

- **Quantum Superposition**: According to Orch-OR, quantum superpositions within the brain's microtubules allow for simultaneous processing of multiple potential conscious states. These superpositions collapse into a singular conscious experience through a process called "objective reduction," orchestrated by neural activity in the brain.
- **Objective Reduction**: This refers to the idea that quantum superpositions collapse not because of external observation, but due to an intrinsic instability in the quantum state itself, a process thought to generate conscious experience.

Microtubules and the Brain

Microtubules are cylindrical structures found in neurons and other cells. In Orch-OR, they are proposed to be the sites where quantum processing occurs, central to the creation of consciousness.

- **Quantum Computation in Microtubules**: Penrose and Hameroff propose that microtubules engage in quantum computation, fundamentally different from classical neural computation. This quantum activity is believed to contribute to conscious experience.
- **Orchestration of Quantum States**: The "orchestrated" part of Orch-OR suggests that the brain's neural networks direct the quantum processes in microtubules, leading to the collapse of quantum superpositions, resulting in consciousness.

Non-Algorithmic Consciousness

Orch-OR posits that consciousness cannot be entirely explained by traditional computational models. Penrose argues that conscious thought involves non-computable processes, which cannot be replicated by standard algorithms.

- **Gödel's Incompleteness Theorem**: Penrose applies Gödel's theorem, which states that within any formal system, there are truths that cannot be proven within that system. He extends this to consciousness, arguing that human cognition involves insights beyond what algorithms can derive, suggesting that quantum processes provide a non-algorithmic foundation for consciousness.

Advantages of Orch-OR in Explaining Consciousness

Addressing the Hard Problem of Consciousness

Orch-OR offers a new perspective on the "hard problem" of consciousness, proposing that quantum processes, which behave differently from classical physics, might explain how subjective experience emerges from physical matter. It provides a potential bridge for understanding the gap between neural processes and conscious experience.

Integration of Quantum Mechanics

By incorporating quantum mechanics into the study of consciousness, Orch-OR opens the door to exploring new dimensions of the mind. Quantum mechanics has successfully explained phenomena beyond the scope of classical physics, and

Orch-OR suggests that consciousness, too, may require a quantum-level explanation.

Non-Computability and Human Cognition

Orch-OR's emphasis on the non-algorithmic aspects of consciousness resonates with the intuition that human thought transcends simple computational processes. It challenges the view that the brain functions purely as a biological computer, offering a more nuanced perspective on the complexity of consciousness.

Relevance to Anesthesia and Consciousness

Hameroff's background in anesthesiology ties Orch-OR to real-world observations about consciousness. Anesthetics, which are known to disrupt consciousness, act on microtubules, lending some support to the idea that these structures are essential to the generation of conscious experience.

Limitations of Orch-OR in Explaining Consciousness

Lack of Empirical Evidence

One of the primary criticisms of Orch-OR is the absence of empirical evidence demonstrating that quantum processes within microtubules generate consciousness. While microtubules are crucial for cellular function, there is little direct evidence to suggest they are involved in quantum computation or conscious experience.

Quantum Decoherence

The phenomenon of quantum decoherence, where quantum states lose their coherence due to interaction with the environment, presents a major challenge for Orch-OR. Critics argue that the brain's "warm and wet" environment is unsuitable for sustaining quantum coherence long enough to influence consciousness.

Complexity and Testability

Orch-OR is a highly complex theory, making it difficult to test empirically. The notion that quantum processes in microtubules contribute to consciousness remains speculative, and designing experiments to verify or refute the theory is challenging.

Reception in the Scientific Community

Orch-OR has been met with skepticism by much of the scientific community. While the theory is innovative, many scientists regard it as speculative due to the lack of supporting evidence and its departure from more traditional views of consciousness, leading to its marginalization within mainstream neuroscience.

Orch-OR and Paranormal Phenomena

Orch-OR opens up intriguing possibilities for explaining certain paranormal phenomena, especially those suggesting that consciousness might extend beyond the physical brain.

- **Near-Death Experiences (NDEs)**: Orch-OR offers a potential framework for understanding NDEs, where individuals report vivid conscious experiences during periods of minimal brain activity. If quantum processes play a role in consciousness, they could manifest uniquely

during these experiences, possibly continuing even when typical brain activity is reduced.
- **Telepathy and Quantum Entanglement**: The concept of quantum entanglement, where particles are connected regardless of distance, might provide a theoretical basis for telepathy or other forms of extrasensory perception. Orch-OR's integration of quantum mechanics into consciousness suggests that entanglement might facilitate non-local communication between conscious minds.
- **Consciousness Beyond the Brain**: Orch-OR raises the possibility that consciousness may not be confined to the brain. It could exist in the quantum realm, interacting with the environment or even persisting after death, which might explain phenomena such as out-of-body experiences or mediumship, where consciousness appears to operate independently of the body.

Conclusion: The Role of Orch-OR in Consciousness Research

Orchestrated Objective Reduction (Orch-OR) offers a bold and unconventional approach to consciousness by proposing that quantum processes within the brain's microtubules generate conscious experience. By merging quantum mechanics with neuroscience, Orch-OR presents a potential solution to the hard problem of consciousness and challenges reductionist views that consciousness can be fully explained by classical neural activity.

However, Orch-OR faces considerable challenges, including the lack of empirical evidence, the issue of quantum decoherence, and skepticism from the scientific community. Despite these hurdles, the theory continues to inspire dialogue and research, especially in areas where traditional theories struggle to explain consciousness.

Orch-OR's potential to explain paranormal phenomena adds an exciting dimension to the theory, suggesting that quantum processes could underpin experiences that transcend conventional scientific understanding. As we deepen our exploration of consciousness, Orch-OR provides a thought-provoking and innovative perspective that broadens our understanding of the mind's possibilities.

https://www.sciencedirect.com/science/article/pii/S1571064513001188

INTEGRATED THEORIES

INTEGRATED INFORMATION THEORY (IIT) AND CONSCIOUSNESS

Introduction: The Emergence of Integrated Information Theory

Integrated Information Theory (IIT) is one of the most sophisticated and influential theories of consciousness developed in recent years. Proposed by neuroscientist Giulio Tononi, IIT seeks to define and measure consciousness in terms of a system's capacity to integrate information. Unlike traditional materialistic theories, which focus primarily on physical processes in the brain, IIT combines materialism with a broader understanding of information, offering a unique perspective on how consciousness arises and what it means.

This chapter explores the core concepts of IIT, its implications for understanding consciousness, and its strengths and limitations, particularly in relation to both scientific inquiry and the exploration of paranormal phenomena.

The Core Concepts of Integrated Information Theory

Consciousness as Integrated Information

At the heart of IIT is the idea that consciousness is intrinsically linked to the ability of a system to integrate information. According to IIT, consciousness is not merely a byproduct of brain activity but a fundamental property of any system that possesses a high degree of integrated information.

- **Integrated Information (Φ)**: IIT introduces the concept of Φ (Phi), a quantitative measure of a system's capacity to integrate information. The higher the Φ, the more integrated the information within the system, and the greater the level of consciousness. A system with a high Φ has many parts that are highly interdependent, meaning that the information processed by the system is deeply interconnected.
- **Irreducibility**: A key idea in IIT is that consciousness corresponds to a system's ability to generate information that cannot be reduced to the sum of its parts. In other words, the whole is greater than the sum of its parts, and this irreducibility is what gives rise to conscious experience.

The Five Axioms of IIT

IIT is built on five foundational axioms, which are intended to capture the essential properties of conscious experience:

1. **Existence**: Consciousness exists and is real; it is an undeniable aspect of experience.

2. **Composition**: Consciousness is structured; it consists of a complex set of interrelated experiences or "concepts."
3. **Information**: Consciousness is informative; every conscious experience is distinct from others, providing unique information.
4. **Integration**: Consciousness is unified; it is experienced as a whole, where different components are integrated into a single experience.
5. **Exclusion**: Consciousness is definite; at any given time, only one specific set of experiences or information is consciously experienced, to the exclusion of all others.

These axioms serve as the basis for IIT's theoretical framework, guiding the development of the theory and its application to various systems, including the human brain.

The Brain as an Integrated Information System

IIT posits that the brain is a highly complex information-processing system that generates consciousness by integrating vast amounts of information across its neural networks. According to IIT:

- **Neural Correlates of Consciousness**: Certain regions of the brain, particularly those involved in high-level cognitive functions (e.g., the cerebral cortex), are likely to have high Φ values, meaning they play a significant role in generating consciousness.
- **Consciousness as a Spectrum**: IIT suggests that consciousness exists on a spectrum, with different systems (including animals, artificial systems, and even simpler organisms) possessing varying degrees of

consciousness depending on their capacity to integrate information.

Pros of Integrated Information Theory in Explaining Consciousness

IIT offers several strengths that make it a compelling theory for understanding consciousness:

Quantifiable and Testable

One of the significant advantages of IIT is that it provides a quantifiable measure of consciousness (Φ), which can, in theory, be tested and measured. This makes IIT particularly appealing to neuroscientists and researchers seeking empirical ways to study consciousness.

Comprehensive and Unifying Framework

IIT offers a comprehensive and unifying framework that explains consciousness across different systems, from simple organisms to complex human brains. By focusing on the integration of information, IIT can potentially explain why certain brain regions contribute more to consciousness than others and why certain brain states are associated with different levels of conscious experience.

Alignment with Empirical Evidence

IIT aligns well with a growing body of empirical evidence from neuroscience. For example, studies have shown that regions of the brain involved in consciousness tend to exhibit high levels of neural integration, consistent with the predictions of IIT.

Additionally, the theory's emphasis on the importance of information processing resonates with current understanding in cognitive science and artificial intelligence.

Applicability Beyond Biology

IIT's framework is not limited to biological systems; it can be applied to any system capable of integrating information. This opens up the possibility of studying consciousness in non-human animals, artificial intelligence, and even hypothetical alien life forms, providing a versatile tool for exploring consciousness in diverse contexts.

CONS OF INTEGRATED INFORMATION THEORY IN EXPLAINING CONSCIOUSNESS

Despite its strengths, IIT faces several significant challenges and criticisms:

Complexity and Practical Challenges

While IIT provides a quantifiable measure of consciousness, calculating Φ for complex systems like the human brain is an extraordinarily challenging task. The sheer complexity of the brain's neural networks makes it difficult to measure Φ accurately, limiting the practical applicability of the theory.

The Explanatory Gap

Like other materialistic theories, IIT faces the "explanatory gap" problem—how does the integration of information lead to the subjective experience of consciousness? While IIT offers a sophisticated model of consciousness, it still struggles to explain why and how integrated information results in the feeling of being conscious.

The Combination Problem

Similar to panpsychism, IIT must address the combination problem—how individual pieces of information or experiences combine to form a unified conscious experience. While IIT posits that consciousness is the result of integrated information, it does not fully explain the mechanisms by which individual components combine into a single, cohesive experience.

Potential Overreach

Some critics argue that IIT might overextend its reach by applying the concept of consciousness to systems that may not genuinely possess it. For example, attributing some level of consciousness to highly integrated artificial systems (such as certain AI models) raises philosophical and ethical questions about what it truly means to be conscious.

Integrated Information Theory and Paranormal Phenomena

IIT offers interesting implications for the study of paranormal phenomena, particularly those that involve non-traditional forms of consciousness:

Non-Human Consciousness

IIT's broad applicability to various systems suggests that consciousness might exist in non-human entities, potentially including animals, plants, and even artificial systems. This opens the door to exploring paranormal phenomena that involve communication or interaction with non-human consciousness, such as animal telepathy or the idea of intelligent plant life.

Consciousness Beyond the Human Brain

If consciousness is a function of integrated information, then it might not be limited to the human brain. IIT could potentially explain phenomena like near-death experiences (NDEs) or out-of-body experiences (OBEs), where consciousness appears to transcend the physical brain. If consciousness is tied to information processing, it might persist or re-emerge in different forms or systems, even outside the human body.

Artificial Intelligence and Consciousness

IIT's implications for artificial intelligence are profound. If AI systems reach a level of integration sufficient to generate a high Φ value, they might be considered conscious according to IIT. This raises questions about the nature of machine consciousness and the possibility of AI systems experiencing consciousness in ways that are currently beyond our understanding.

CONCLUSION: THE ROLE OF INTEGRATED INFORMATION THEORY IN CONSCIOUSNESS RESEARCH

Integrated Information Theory (IIT) offers a groundbreaking approach to understanding consciousness, proposing that the capacity to integrate information is the key to generating conscious experience. By providing a quantifiable measure of consciousness, IIT bridges the gap between materialistic neuroscience and a broader understanding of information, offering a unifying framework for studying consciousness across different systems.

However, IIT also faces significant challenges, particularly in addressing the explanatory gap and the combination problem. Its complexity and the difficulty of measuring Φ in real-world systems present practical obstacles, and its application to non-human and artificial systems raises philosophical and ethical questions.

Despite these challenges, IIT remains one of the most promising and innovative theories in consciousness research, with the potential to expand our understanding of consciousness in ways that could reshape both scientific inquiry and our approach to paranormal phenomena. As we continue to explore the mysteries of consciousness, IIT provides a valuable tool for investigating how information and experience intertwine to create the rich tapestry of conscious life.

As we conclude our exploration of the myriad theories of consciousness, it becomes evident that while each offers valuable insights, none fully encapsulates the enigmatic phenomena often observed in paranormal studies. Materialistic theories, with their reliance on physical processes and neural correlates, provide a robust framework for understanding consciousness as a product of brain activity. Yet, they fall short in explaining experiences that transcend the known capabilities of the human mind, such as telepathy, precognition, or encounters with otherworldly entities.

Philosophical perspectives, from dualism to panpsychism, challenge the reductionist view by suggesting that consciousness might be more than just a byproduct of physical processes. These theories open the door to considering consciousness as a fundamental aspect of reality, potentially bridging the gap between the material and the mystical. However, they often lack empirical grounding, leaving them vulnerable to skepticism from the scientific community.Integrative and esoteric models, like Integrated Information Theory and Orchestrated Objective Reduction, attempt to synthesize materialistic and non-materialistic views. They propose that consciousness might arise from complex information integration or even quantum processes. Yet, these theories remain speculative and have yet to provide definitive explanations for the paranormal phenomena that intrigue researchers and laypeople alike.

The persistent inability of these theories to fully account for paranormal experiences suggests a need for science to broaden its horizons. The scientific method, with its emphasis on empirical evidence and reproducibility, is a powerful tool for understanding the natural world. However, it can also be limiting when faced with phenomena that defy conventional explanation. To truly advance our understanding of consciousness and the paranormal, science must be willing to entertain possibilities that lie beyond its current paradigms.

This does not mean abandoning rigorous scientific principles but rather expanding them to include interdisciplinary approaches and open-minded inquiry. By fostering a dialogue between science, philosophy, and even spirituality, we can begin to construct a more comprehensive framework that acknowledges the complexity and mystery of consciousness. In doing so, we may uncover new insights into the nature of reality itself, bridging the gap between the known and the unknown, and shedding light on the profound mysteries that continue to elude us.In conclusion, while current theories of consciousness offer valuable perspectives, they remain incomplete in addressing the full spectrum of human experience. As we venture into the uncharted territories of the mind, it is imperative that science remains open to the unknown, embracing the possibility that the answers we seek may lie beyond the limits of our current understanding. Only then can we hope to unravel the true nature of consciousness and its connection to the paranormal

COSMIC ENTITIES

Donald Hoffman, a cognitive scientist and professor at the University of California, Irvine, is known for his groundbreaking work on the nature of perception and reality. Hoffman challenges the conventional view that our senses provide a true representation of the world around us. Instead, he proposes that what we perceive is not reality itself, but a user interface designed by evolution to help us survive. This theory, known as the Interface Theory of Perception, suggests that our perceptions are more akin to icons on a computer screen, which simplify and hide the complex workings beneath.

Hoffman's work has profound implications for our understanding of consciousness and reality, particularly in relation to paranormal phenomena. If our perceptions are not a direct reflection of reality, then experiences that are typically dismissed as "paranormal" may not be as easily discounted. This chapter explores Hoffman's theories in detail and considers how they might provide a new framework for understanding phenomena such as Out-of-Body Experiences (OBEs), Remote Viewing, and other paranormal events.

THE INTERFACE THEORY OF PERCEPTION

The Evolutionary Basis

Hoffman's Interface Theory of Perception is rooted in evolutionary biology. He argues that natural selection favors perceptions that enhance survival and reproduction, not necessarily those that provide an accurate depiction of reality.

- **Perception as a User Interface**: According to Hoffman, our sensory experiences are like a user interface on a computer, designed to present information in a way that is useful, rather than true. For example, just as a computer icon represents a file without revealing its complex internal structure, our perception of a tree, for instance, is a simplified representation of a far more complex reality.
- **Survival Over Truth**: Hoffman's theory suggests that organisms that perceive reality "as it is" are not necessarily more likely to survive. Instead, those that develop perceptions that are useful for survival—regardless of their accuracy—are more likely to pass on their genes. Thus, our perceptions are shaped by evolutionary pressures to ensure survival, not to reveal the true nature of reality.

Conscious Realism

Building on the Interface Theory, Hoffman introduces the concept of "Conscious Realism," which posits that consciousness is the fundamental reality, not physical objects.

- **Consciousness as Primary**: In Hoffman's view, what we consider physical reality is actually a construct of conscious agents. These agents interact with each other through an interface that we perceive as the physical world. Therefore, consciousness is the foundation of everything, and what we perceive as material objects are simply representations created by consciousness.
- **Physical Objects as Symbols**: Just as icons on a desktop are not the actual files but symbols representing them,

physical objects are symbols created by consciousness to interact with other conscious agents. This theory challenges the materialist view that consciousness arises from physical matter, suggesting instead that consciousness creates the experience of matter.

Implications for Paranormal Phenomena

Hoffman's theories offer a radically different perspective on reality that has significant implications for understanding paranormal phenomena. If our perceptions are not a true reflection of reality, then experiences that seem to defy physical laws might be glimpses of a deeper, underlying reality that our "interface" is not fully equipped to interpret.

Out-of-Body Experiences (OBEs) and Hoffman's Interface

Out-of-Body Experiences (OBEs), where individuals perceive themselves as existing outside their physical body, are often dismissed as hallucinations or neurological anomalies. However, Hoffman's Interface Theory provides a different interpretation.

- **Beyond the Interface**: According to Hoffman, OBEs might represent moments when the usual "interface" that governs our perception is disrupted, allowing consciousness to access information or perspectives outside the normal sensory bounds. This could explain why individuals experiencing OBEs often report vivid, detailed perceptions of their surroundings from a perspective outside their body.
- **Perception of Non-Local Consciousness**: If consciousness is not bound by the physical body, as Hoffman suggests,

OBEs could be instances where individuals temporarily step outside the usual constraints of their user interface, perceiving a broader reality that is normally hidden from view.

Remote Viewing and the Nature of Perception

Remote Viewing, the ability to perceive distant or unseen locations using extrasensory perception (ESP), also aligns with Hoffman's theories.

- **Accessing Hidden Realities**: If our senses are designed to simplify and hide the true complexity of reality, as Hoffman proposes, then Remote Viewing might involve accessing information that is typically hidden by our interface. This could explain why remote viewers can sometimes accurately describe locations they have never physically visited.
- **Non-Local Interaction**: Hoffman's idea that consciousness is the fundamental reality suggests that Remote Viewing could involve direct interaction between conscious agents, bypassing the physical constraints of distance and time that normally govern our perceptions.

Apparitions and Entities: Icons of Consciousness?

Apparitions, ghosts, and other entities reported in paranormal experiences could be interpreted through Hoffman's lens as icons or representations created by consciousness.

- **Manifestations of Conscious Agents**: If what we perceive as physical entities are merely symbols created by consciousness, then apparitions might be

representations of other conscious agents that exist beyond our normal sensory interface. These entities might not be bound by the same physical laws that govern our everyday experiences, leading to their classification as "paranormal."
- **Distortions or Glimpses of Reality?**: Apparitions might be perceived when the usual interface is disrupted or altered, allowing individuals to perceive aspects of reality that are normally filtered out. These experiences might not be distortions or errors, but rather genuine interactions with other conscious agents that our interface usually hides.

Near-Death Experiences (NDEs) and the Transition of Consciousness

Near-Death Experiences (NDEs), where individuals report profound experiences during moments of clinical death, often include elements that seem to transcend physical reality, such as traveling through tunnels of light or encountering deceased loved ones.

- **Beyond the Physical Interface**: Hoffman's theories suggest that NDEs might occur when the physical interface begins to shut down, allowing consciousness to perceive a different level of reality. The common elements of NDEs, such as the tunnel of light or feelings of peace, could be part of a different interface that consciousness interacts with as it transitions away from the physical body.
- **The Continuity of Consciousness**: Hoffman's Conscious Realism implies that consciousness does not cease with

the death of the physical body. NDEs might therefore represent a transition to a different state of awareness, one that is not bound by the physical interface we experience in life.

Challenges and Criticisms

While Hoffman's theories offer intriguing possibilities for understanding paranormal phenomena, they are not without challenges and criticisms.

Scientific Acceptance

One of the primary challenges to Hoffman's theories is the lack of empirical evidence that can be tested and validated within the framework of traditional science.

- **Falsifiability**: Critics argue that Hoffman's theories, particularly Conscious Realism, are difficult to test or falsify using conventional scientific methods. This makes it challenging to assess their validity in the context of established scientific principles.
- **Interdisciplinary Resistance**: Hoffman's ideas challenge fundamental assumptions in both neuroscience and physics, leading to resistance from those who adhere to materialistic explanations of consciousness. Integrating these theories with existing scientific knowledge requires a significant shift in perspective that many scientists are hesitant to make.

1Interpretative Flexibility

Hoffman's theories are open to a wide range of interpretations, which can make them difficult to apply consistently to specific phenomena.

- **Multiple Explanations**: Because Hoffman's ideas are based on the notion that our perceptions are not direct reflections of reality, they can be used to explain a wide variety of experiences, both normal and paranormal. This flexibility, while intriguing, can also make the theories seem overly broad or unfalsifiable.
- **Philosophical Implications**: Hoffman's theories have significant philosophical implications, particularly regarding the nature of reality and the role of consciousness. While this makes them valuable for theoretical exploration, it also places them at the intersection of science and philosophy, where empirical validation is more complex.

The Potential of Hoffman's Theories for Paranormal Research

Despite the challenges, Hoffman's Interface Theory and Conscious Realism provide a valuable framework for exploring paranormal phenomena in a new light.

A New Paradigm for Consciousness

Hoffman's work encourages a shift away from materialistic explanations of consciousness, suggesting instead that consciousness is the foundation of reality. This paradigm opens the door to a more inclusive understanding of experiences that fall outside conventional scientific explanations.

- **Expanding Research Horizons**: By considering consciousness as primary, researchers can explore paranormal phenomena without the constraints of materialistic assumptions. This could lead to new insights and discoveries that bridge the gap between science and experiences traditionally labeled as "paranormal."
- **Integrating Science and Spirituality**: Hoffman's theories offer a potential bridge between scientific inquiry and spiritual or metaphysical perspectives, allowing for a more holistic approach to understanding consciousness and reality.

Practical Applications in Investigating Paranormal Phenomena

Hoffman's ideas could inspire new methodologies and approaches to investigating paranormal phenomena.

- **Innovative Research Designs**: Researchers might develop experiments that test the limits of perception and consciousness, using Hoffman's theories as a basis for understanding how and why certain phenomena occur.
- **Reevaluating Historical Accounts**: Historical and anecdotal reports of paranormal experiences could be reevaluated in light of Hoffman's theories, providing new interpretations and insights that align with the idea of consciousness as a fundamental aspect of reality.

Conclusion: Reimagining Reality Through Hoffman's Lens

Donald Hoffman's Interface Theory of Perception and Conscious Realism offer a revolutionary way of understanding consciousness, reality, and the nature of human experience. By proposing that our perceptions are not a direct reflection of reality but a simplified interface, Hoffman challenges us to reconsider the very fabric of what we consider "real."

In the context of paranormal phenomena, Hoffman's theories provide a powerful framework for interpreting experiences that defy conventional explanations. Out-of-Body Experiences, Remote Viewing, apparitions, and Near-Death Experiences may all be understood as moments when the usual interface of perception is altered or transcended, allowing consciousness to interact with a deeper, more complex reality.

While Hoffman's ideas are still in the early stages of acceptance within the scientific community, their potential to reshape our understanding of consciousness and reality cannot be ignored. As research continues to evolve, Hoffman's theories may play a crucial role in bridging the gap between science and the paranormal, offering new insights into the mysteries that have fascinated humanity for centuries. By reimagining reality through Hoffman's lens, we open ourselves to the possibility that consciousness is not just a product of the brain, but the fundamental essence of the universe itself.

THE INTERSECTION OF SCIENCE AND THE UNEXPLAINED

The Role of Science in Modern Life

Science has undeniably shaped the world we live in today. From the internet that connects us globally to the smartphones we use to communicate with loved ones across the planet, scientific progress has revolutionized our daily lives. It has provided us with unprecedented access to information, technology, and convenience, making our modern way of life possible.

The Limitations of a Purely Scientific Approach

However, in this age of scientific advancement, it is easy to become overly fixated on the power of science, to the point where the very process that has brought us this far may now be limiting our understanding of the world. When faced with life's great questions, it becomes clear that a purely scientific approach may not be sufficient to provide all the answers we seek.

Embracing a Balanced Perspective

To truly unravel the mysteries of our existence, we must adopt a balanced perspective that combines the rigorous, analytical thinking of science with an openness to phenomena that science has yet to fully explain. By acknowledging the countless reports of strange experiences and unexplained events that have been documented throughout history, we can begin to explore new avenues of understanding.

Exploring the Unexplained

In the coming chapters, we will delve into these fascinating phenomena that have long perplexed scientists and laypeople alike. From near-death experiences and out-of-body adventures to past-life memories and other inexplicable occurrences, we will examine these mysteries with a discerning eye, seeking to uncover the truths that lie beneath the surface.

Bridging the Gap Between Science and Experience

By approaching these enigmas with a mix of scientific inquiry and open-mindedness, we can begin to bridge the gap between the known and the unknown. We must recognize that science, while a powerful tool, is ultimately wielded by human minds and is therefore subject to the same limitations and biases that we all possess.

Expanding the Boundaries of Understanding

As we explore these strange phenomena, we may find that the answers to life's greatest questions lie not solely in the domain of science but in the rich tapestry of human experience that has been woven throughout the ages. By embracing this broader perspective and investigating these mysteries with curiosity and discernment, we can expand the boundaries of our understanding and catch a glimpse of the profound truths that underlie our existence.

GLIMPSE INTO THE UNKNOWN

Throughout history, countless individuals across cultures and time periods have reported experiences that defy conventional scientific explanations. These experiences are often dismissed by mainstream science as anecdotal or the result of psychological or physiological processes. However, when considered collectively and in depth, they form a body of evidence that demands our attention. The phenomena discussed in this book include:

1. Ghosts and Apparitions:
Ghosts and apparitions are perhaps the most widely recognized paranormal phenomena. These are visual or auditory manifestations that appear to represent deceased individuals, often in locations with a significant emotional or historical connection. The widespread nature of these reports across cultures and history, along with documented cases that defy easy explanation, make them a significant area of study in the exploration of life after death.

2. Near-Death Experiences (NDEs):
Near-death experiences are among the most widely reported and studied phenomena related to the afterlife. Individuals who have been on the brink of death often report vivid experiences that include feelings of peace, out-of-body experiences, encounters with deceased loved ones, and visions of a bright light or otherworldly realms. These experiences are strikingly similar across different cultures and backgrounds, suggesting a universal aspect of human consciousness that might persist beyond death. The question of whether these experiences are mere byproducts of a dying brain or glimpses into an afterlife is central to our inquiry.

2. Out-of-Body Experiences (OBEs):

Related to NDEs, out-of-body experiences occur when individuals perceive themselves as being outside of their physical bodies, often observing their surroundings from a different vantage point. OBEs can occur spontaneously, during meditation, or in near-death situations. What makes OBEs particularly intriguing is that individuals sometimes report accurate details about their environment that they could not have known from their physical perspective, suggesting that consciousness might be able to detach from the physical body and operate independently.

3. Reincarnation:
Another phenomenon that challenges our understanding of consciousness is the recall of past-life memories, particularly in young children. These children often recount detailed memories of lives they have never lived, sometimes providing information that can be historically verified. The existence of past-life memories raises profound questions about the nature of the soul, reincarnation, and the continuity of consciousness across different lifetimes.

4. Mediumship and Communication with the Deceased:
Mediums claim to communicate with the spirits of the deceased, conveying messages that are often personal and specific to the individuals they are communicating with. While skepticism abounds, there have been instances where mediums have provided information that they could not have known through normal means, suggesting the possibility that consciousness continues to exist after death and can interact with the living.

7. Deathbed Visions and Shared Death Experiences:

Deathbed visions occur when individuals nearing death report seeing deceased loved ones, religious figures, or other comforting presences. These visions are often accompanied by a sense of peace and acceptance. Shared death experiences, on the other hand, are reported by people who are present at the moment of someone else's death and who experience similar phenomena, such as seeing a light or feeling a sense of euphoria. Both types of experiences suggest that there may be a transitional phase of consciousness as the soul prepares to leave the physical body.

The Significance of These Phenomena

Each of these phenomena, when considered in isolation, might be explained away by skeptics as psychological anomalies, misinterpretations, or even outright fabrications. However, when viewed collectively, they form a compelling body of evidence that challenges the materialist view of consciousness. If we accept that these phenomena are not merely the products of a dying brain or overactive imagination, then we must consider the possibility that they provide glimpses into a reality that extends beyond the physical world.

These phenomena are important not only because they suggest the survival of consciousness after death, but also because they compel us to rethink our understanding of what it means to be conscious. Modern science has made great strides in understanding the brain and its functions, but consciousness itself remains one of the greatest mysteries. Is consciousness merely an emergent property of brain activity, or is it something more—something that transcends the physical body and perhaps even the physical universe?

By exploring these phenomena, we are also engaging in a broader inquiry into the nature of reality itself. If consciousness can exist independently of the body, what does that mean for our understanding of the universe? Are there dimensions of existence beyond the material? Are there forces or energies that we have yet to discover? These are the questions that lie at the heart of this book.

As we move forward in our exploration, we will begin by examining one of the most enduring and widespread phenomena associated with the afterlife: ghosts and apparitions. These entities have been reported throughout history and across cultures, often in ways that are strikingly consistent. Whether they are the spirits of the deceased, imprints of past events, or something else entirely, ghosts and apparitions offer a fascinating window into the possibility that consciousness can persist after death.

In the next chapter, we will delve into the history of ghost sightings, examine notable cases, and explore the various theories that have been proposed to explain these mysterious occurrences. We will also consider the scientific investigations that have been conducted, as well as the limitations of these studies in fully capturing the essence of what people experience. By doing so, we will set the stage for a deeper understanding of how ghosts and apparitions fit into the broader question of life after death.

As you turn the page, prepare to step into a world where the past meets the present, where the seen and the unseen converge, and where the possibility of life beyond death takes on a tangible form. Whether you approach these stories with skepticism or belief, they provide an essential piece of the puzzle in our quest to understand the nature of consciousness and what might await us beyond this life.

GHOSTS AND APPARITIONS

INTRODUCTION

The fascination with ghosts and apparitions has spanned centuries, capturing the human imagination and fueling countless stories, legends, and personal accounts. While these spectral encounters have often been relegated to the realms of folklore and superstition, the persistence of ghostly phenomena across cultures and historical periods demands a closer examination. This chapter embarks on a journey through the mysterious world of ghosts and apparitions, exploring whether these experiences might provide compelling evidence for the existence of an afterlife.

The primary purpose of this chapter is to examine different types of ghostly phenomena and analyze their potential connection to the survival of consciousness beyond death. By exploring these manifestations through a lens of open-minded inquiry, we aim to present a balanced view that neither blindly accepts nor dismisses the possibility of an afterlife. Instead, we will evaluate the evidence through case studies, eyewitness accounts, and scientific theories, considering how these phenomena might fit into a broader understanding of life, death, and the persistence of consciousness.

Central to this discussion is the idea that energy and consciousness may persist beyond physical death. This concept, while still a topic of debate among scientists and philosophers, provides a framework for understanding how ghosts and apparitions might be more than mere figments of imagination or psychological anomalies. By delving into this possibility, we can begin to explore the implications of such persistence, not only for the individuals who experience these phenomena but also for our collective understanding of what it means to live, die, and potentially continue existing in another form.

The chapter will be structured to first define and categorize the different types of ghosts, including residual ghosts, intelligent spirits, and poltergeists. Each category will be supported by specific examples and case studies, illustrating the unique characteristics and behaviors associated with these entities. Additionally, we will delve into theories that attempt to explain these phenomena, such as the Stone Tape Theory for residual hauntings and psychokinesis in the case of poltergeists.

As we progress, we will address the broader question of whether these ghostly encounters can be seen as evidence for an afterlife. The chapter will conclude with a discussion of the implications of such evidence, encouraging readers to consider the persistence of energy and consciousness as a potential reality. By approaching the topic with an open yet critical mind, this chapter aims to contribute to the ongoing conversation about life after death and the nature of existence itself.

TYPES OF GHOSTS
RESIDUAL GHOSTS

When discussing the types of ghosts, it is essential to start with one of the most frequently reported and yet enigmatic forms: residual ghosts. These entities differ significantly from other types of ghostly manifestations in that they are not considered to be conscious or aware of their surroundings. Instead, they are often described as imprints or recordings of past events that replay in specific locations, typically where intense emotional or traumatic events have occurred or where someone repeated the same activity day after day like sitting in a jail cell or doing day to day tasks. The idea behind residual ghosts suggests that some environments can absorb and later replay the energies associated with events, much like a video recording that replays without any awareness or interaction from the "recorded" individuals.

The concept of residual hauntings aligns with a theory known as the Stone Tape Theory, which posits that materials like stone, wood, and other elements of the environment can somehow capture and store energy from emotionally charged events. This energy is then believed to replay periodically under certain conditions, creating the phenomenon we recognize as a residual ghost. Unlike intelligent spirits, which may interact with the living, residual ghosts are thought to follow a predetermined script, re-enacting the same scene repeatedly without deviation, interaction, or awareness.

THE STONE TAPE THEORY: RECORDING AND PLAYBACK

The Stone Tape Theory emerged in the 20th century as a possible explanation for why certain locations seem to be more haunted than others. According to this theory, the environment can act as a sort of recording medium, capturing the energy of intense human emotions and experiences, particularly those associated with trauma, violence, or deep emotional resonance. According to the stone tape theory, the energy from a significant event is believed to be "recorded" in the surrounding materials, often natural elements like stone, at the precise moment the event takes place. This stored energy can later be "replayed" under the right conditions, manifesting as the ghostly phenomena experienced by people in the area.

However, I have a different perspective on this concept. Rather than the surrounding materials capturing the imprint, I believe that the very fabric of space-time itself acts as a storage medium for this information. The idea is that space-time, the fundamental structure of the universe, has the capacity to store and preserve the energy and information associated with events that occur within it.

This suggests that ghostly apparitions and other paranormal occurrences could be the result of space-time itself "playing back" the recorded information, rather than the phenomena being tied to specific materials in the environment. This theory opens up fascinating possibilities about the nature of the universe and how it interacts with the events that transpire within it, potentially offering a new way to understand and investigate paranormal experiences.

While the Stone Tape Theory is largely speculative and lacks empirical evidence, it does offer a framework for understanding why some hauntings are repetitive and non-interactive. Proponents of this theory suggest that just as a tape recorder captures and replays sound, the environment may capture and replay visual and auditory experiences, particularly those associated with significant emotional or traumatic events or repeated events. The idea here is not that a ghostly spirit is present in the traditional sense, but rather that the environment is replaying a "recording" of past events.

CHARACTERISTICS OF RESIDUAL HAUNTINGS

Residual hauntings exhibit several distinct characteristics that set them apart from other types of ghostly phenomena. First and foremost, they are repetitive. Witnesses often report seeing the same apparition performing the same actions over and over again, usually without any variation. For example, a common report might involve a ghostly figure walking down a hallway, disappearing through a door that no longer exists, or re-enacting a dramatic event such as a battle or a murder.

One of the most intriguing aspects of residual hauntings is that the ghostly figures involved often seem completely unaware of their surroundings. They do not interact with witnesses, nor do they acknowledge the presence of the living. This lack of interaction strongly suggests that these apparitions are not conscious entities but rather recordings or imprints of past events.

Another key feature of residual hauntings is their strong association with specific locations. These locations are often places where traumatic or emotionally charged events have occurred. For instance, many battlefields, such as Gettysburg in the United States, are famous for their residual hauntings. Visitors to these sites often report hearing the sounds of battle—gunfire, shouting, and the clash of metal—long after the actual events have ceased. Similarly, many haunted houses are said to replay scenes of domestic tragedy, such as the ghost of a woman endlessly searching for her lost child or a figure descending a staircase.

The predictability and repetitive nature of residual hauntings suggest that these ghosts are not active spirits but rather energy imprints that have been left behind in the environment. This energy, stored in the fabric of the building or landscape, is released under certain conditions, creating the phenomenon of a residual ghost.

Examples of Residual Hauntings

There are numerous documented cases of residual hauntings, each providing unique insights into the nature of this phenomenon. One of the most famous examples is the ghostly apparitions of Roman soldiers seen in the cellar of the Treasurer's House in York, England.
In 1953, a young apprentice plumber named Harry Martindale was working in the cellar when he claimed to see a group of Roman soldiers emerge from a wall. The soldiers were dressed in full Roman military attire, but what struck Martindale as particularly strange was that they appeared to be walking on their knees, with the lower half of their legs obscured by the floor. It was later discovered that the original Roman road was located about 18 inches below the current cellar floor, which would explain why the soldiers appeared as they did.

Martindale's account is particularly compelling because he had no prior knowledge of the history of the site or the Roman road. His detailed description of the soldiers, including their armor and weapons, matched historical records, lending credence to his story. Importantly, the soldiers seemed completely unaware of Martindale's presence, supporting the idea that this was a residual haunting—a replay of a past event rather than an encounter with conscious spirits.

Another well-known case involves the Battle of Gettysburg, a site of immense bloodshed during the American Civil War. Visitors to the battlefield have reported seeing ghostly soldiers marching, hearing the sounds of battle, and even smelling gunpowder in the air. These experiences are often described as though they are witnessing a scene from the past unfolding before their eyes, rather than interacting with spirits who are aware of their presence. The residual energy from the intense emotions and violence of the battle seems to have been imprinted on the landscape, replaying itself to those who visit the site.

In some cases, residual hauntings can involve not just visual apparitions but also sounds, smells, and even physical sensations. For example, in haunted theaters, people have reported hearing the sounds of long-ago performances, complete with applause, music, and the hum of the audience. Similarly, in old prisons or hospitals, visitors might hear the echo of footsteps, the clanging of metal doors, or even the distant cries of former inmates or patients.

These examples highlight the wide range of experiences that can fall under the category of residual hauntings. Whether they involve ghostly apparitions, sounds, or other sensory phenomena, these hauntings seem to suggest that the energy of past events can leave a lasting imprint on the environment, capable of being "replayed" long after the original event has passed.

IMPLICATIONS FOR THE CONCEPT OF AN AFTERLIFE

The existence of residual ghosts raises intriguing questions about the nature of consciousness and the possibility of an afterlife. If residual hauntings are indeed energy imprints left behind by emotionally charged events, this could imply that human experiences and emotions have a lasting impact on the environment. However, because these imprints do not appear to involve conscious entities, they may not directly support the idea of a traditional afterlife where the deceased retain awareness and agency.

Instead, residual hauntings might suggest a form of "echo" left behind by powerful emotions and experiences. This idea aligns with certain theories of consciousness that propose the mind or soul can leave behind traces or impressions, even if it does not continue in a fully conscious form after death. While residual hauntings alone may not provide conclusive evidence for an afterlife, they do add a layer of complexity to our understanding of how human energy and experiences interact with the physical world.

INTELLIGENT HAUNTINGS

Intelligent hauntings often referred to as interactive or sentient ghosts, represent a category of ghosts distinct from residual hauntings. Unlike residual ghosts, which are thought to be mere imprints or echoes of past events, intelligent spirits are believed to be the conscious manifestations of deceased individuals who retain awareness of their surroundings and the ability to interact with the living. These entities appear to possess a sense of purpose, often displaying behaviors that suggest they are attempting to communicate, convey messages, or even complete unfinished business from their former lives.

The concept of intelligent spirits is rooted in the belief that consciousness can persist beyond physical death. Proponents of this idea argue that the soul or essence of a person can continue to exist after the body has died, either in a state of limbo, on another plane of existence, or in direct proximity to the world of the living. This persistent consciousness is thought to be responsible for the ghostly activities attributed to intelligent spirits, such as moving objects, creating sounds, manifesting visibly, and, most significantly, engaging with those who are still alive.

CHARACTERISTICS OF INTELLIGENT SPIRITS

Intelligent spirits are often characterized by their ability to communicate with the living in various ways. This communication can take many forms, ranging from subtle signs to more overt actions that leave no doubt about the spirit's awareness and intent. Some of the most common characteristics of intelligent spirits include:

- Communication: One of the hallmark traits of intelligent spirits is their ability to communicate with the living. This communication can occur through a variety of methods, including verbal messages, telepathic impressions, or even writing. For instance, some reports describe spirits leaving handwritten notes or messages on mirrors. In other cases, spirits may communicate through auditory phenomena, such as disembodied voices or distinct sounds like knocking, tapping, or calling out a person's name.

- Movement: Intelligent spirits are also often associated with the movement of objects. This phenomenon, sometimes referred to as apportation, involves the apparent manipulation of physical objects by an unseen force. Objects might be moved from one location to another, doors might open and close by themselves, or personal items might be rearranged in a manner that seems intentional. These actions are typically interpreted as attempts by the spirit to gain attention or convey a message.

- Purposeful Behavior: Unlike residual ghosts, which follow a repetitive pattern without deviation, intelligent spirits exhibit purposeful behavior. They may appear at specific times or in response to particular events or individuals. For example, a spirit might manifest during a family gathering, seemingly to offer comfort or support. In other cases, spirits have been reported to intervene in dangerous situations, such as warning individuals of impending harm or providing guidance during a crisis.

- Recognition and Interaction: Intelligent spirits often demonstrate recognition of individuals, particularly those with whom they had a close relationship during their lifetime. This recognition can manifest in various ways, such as a spirit calling out a person's name, touching them, or even appearing to comfort them during moments of grief or distress. These interactions are typically personal and meaningful, reinforcing the idea that the spirit retains some form of memory and emotional connection.

Examples of Intelligent Spirit Encounters
One of the most famous examples of an intelligent spirit encounter is the case of the Greenbrier Ghost, a well-known story from West Virginia that dates back to the late 19th century. In this case, a woman named Zona Heaster Shue was found dead under mysterious circumstances in 1897. Her death was initially ruled as natural, but her mother, Mary Jane Heaster, believed otherwise. According to Mary Jane, Zona's spirit appeared to her over several nights, revealing that she had been murdered by her husband, Edward Shue. The spirit reportedly provided detailed information about how the murder occurred, including the manner in which her neck was broken.

Mary Jane Heaster took this information to the authorities, who eventually exhumed Zona's body and found evidence consistent with the spirit's account—specifically, that her neck had indeed been broken in a manner suggesting foul play. As a result, Edward Shue was arrested, tried, and convicted of Zona's murder. The Greenbrier Ghost case is often cited as a compelling example of an intelligent spirit providing information that led to real-world consequences, in this case, the conviction of a murderer (https://news.google.com/newspapers?id=o9tdAAAAIBAJ&pg=1068,3035905&dq=shue&hl=en for more information and the original article)

Another notable example is the haunting of the Whaley House in San Diego, California. The Whaley House, built in 1857, is widely regarded as one of the most haunted houses in the United States. Numerous accounts suggest that the spirits of former residents, particularly members of the Whaley family, continue to inhabit the house. Visitors and paranormal investigators have reported a wide range of phenomena, including apparitions, unexplained noises, and the movement of objects. Thomas Whaley, the original owner, is often seen or heard, with reports of his figure appearing at the top of the staircase or the sound of his footsteps echoing through the halls. These experiences are interpreted as evidence of intelligent spirits—entities that are aware of their surroundings and continue to "live" in the house, interacting with those who visit.

In addition to these well-known cases, countless other reports from individuals around the world describe interactions with intelligent spirits. These encounters often occur in private homes, where the spirits of deceased family members are said to linger. For instance, people frequently report seeing or feeling the presence of a recently deceased loved one, particularly in the days or weeks following their death. These experiences often involve the spirit providing comfort or reassurance, such as appearing in dreams, manifesting as a warm, familiar presence, or even leaving behind physical signs like a favorite scent or a familiar object placed in an unexpected location.

Various theories have been proposed to explain the existence of intelligent spirits. One of the most common is the survival hypothesis, which posits that the human soul or consciousness survives bodily death and can continue to interact with the physical world. According to this theory, intelligent spirits are the disembodied consciousnesses of individuals who have passed away but remain connected to the living world, either because they have unfinished business, a strong emotional attachment, or a desire to communicate with loved ones, or simply because they are afraid or unwilling to crossover.

Another theory suggests that intelligent spirits may be manifestations of energy consciousness—the idea that consciousness is a form of energy that can exist independently of the physical body. This theory aligns with certain interpretations of quantum physics, which propose that consciousness might be a fundamental component of the universe, not limited by physical death. In this view, intelligent spirits are expressions of this enduring consciousness, able to interact with the living due to their energy-based nature.

Some researchers also explore the possibility of parallel dimensions or alternate realities as explanations for intelligent spirits. This theory suggests that these spirits exist in a parallel dimension that occasionally overlaps with our own, allowing for interactions between the living and the deceased. In this model, what we perceive as ghosts might actually be glimpses into another dimension where the deceased continue to exist in a state similar to our own.

Implications for the Concept of an Afterlife

The existence of intelligent spirits, if proven beyond anecdotal evidence, would have profound implications for our understanding of life, death, and the nature of consciousness. These spirits suggest that death may not be the end of consciousness, but rather a transition to another state of existence. The ability of these spirits to interact with the living, communicate messages, and even influence the physical world points to a form of survival that transcends the limitations of the physical body.

For many, the idea of intelligent spirits provides comfort and reassurance that death is not the final chapter, but instead a doorway to a new form of existence. It suggests that the bonds of love, memory, and emotion can persist beyond death, allowing for continued interaction between the living and the deceased. This possibility opens up new avenues for exploring the nature of consciousness, the structure of reality, and the potential for an afterlife.

POLTERGEISTS

Definition: "Noisy Ghosts" Characterized by Physical Disturbances

Poltergeists, often referred to as "noisy ghosts," are a unique and particularly unsettling type of paranormal phenomenon. Unlike residual ghosts or intelligent spirits, which may manifest visually or through subtle interactions, poltergeists are characterized by their ability to create significant physical disturbances. These disturbances can range from minor annoyances, such as unexplained knocking or objects moving on their own, to more alarming events like furniture being thrown across a room or appliances turning on and off without explanation. The term "poltergeist" itself is derived from the German words "poltern," meaning "to make noise," and "geist," meaning "spirit" or "ghost."

Poltergeist activity is typically associated with a specific location, often a home, and frequently centers around a particular individual, known as the "agent." This agent is usually an adolescent, most commonly a teenage girl, though cases involving adults and even younger children have also been reported. The disturbances often begin suddenly and can escalate in intensity, sometimes lasting for weeks, months, or even years before stopping just as abruptly as they started. The exact cause of poltergeist activity remains a topic of debate and speculation, with various theories attempting to explain these enigmatic events.

THEORIES: PSYCHOKINESIS (PK)

One of the most widely discussed theories regarding the nature of poltergeists is that they are a manifestation of psychokinesis (PK)—the ability of the mind to influence physical objects without any physical interaction. This theory suggests that the disturbances associated with poltergeist activity are not caused by an external spirit or entity, but rather by the unconscious mind of the agent, typically a person undergoing significant emotional or psychological stress. According to this theory, the stress or emotional turmoil creates a buildup of psychic energy, which is then released in the form of psychokinetic disturbances.

Supporters of the psychokinesis theory point to the frequent association of poltergeist activity with adolescents, a group often experiencing intense emotional and hormonal changes. The idea is that these internal pressures manifest externally in the form of unexplained physical phenomena, such as objects moving, strange noises, and other disturbances. In this view, the agent is not consciously aware of their role in the events and may even be frightened or confused by the activity, just like other witnesses.

Another prominent theory posits that poltergeist activity is caused by mischievous or malevolent entities. Unlike intelligent spirits, which may have clear motivations or communicate directly with the living, these entities are often described as chaotic, playful, or even malicious. In some cultures, they are referred to as trickster spirits, demons, or other supernatural beings that delight in causing confusion, fear, and disruption.

This theory is supported by the often unpredictable and sometimes violent nature of poltergeist phenomena. Objects may be hurled across rooms, fires might spontaneously ignite, and loud, disembodied voices or laughter may be heard. These entities are believed to be drawn to certain locations or individuals, possibly feeding off the fear and energy generated by their disturbances. In some cases, the activity is seen as a form of harassment or punishment, though the reasons for such behavior remain unclear.

While the psychokinesis and mischievous entity theories are the most prevalent, other explanations have been proposed, including the idea that poltergeist activity could be the result of environmental factors, such as electromagnetic disturbances, or even unknown natural phenomena. However, none of these theories have been definitively proven, leaving poltergeists as one of the most mysterious and controversial aspects of paranormal research.

Example: The Enfield Poltergeist
One of the most famous and well-documented cases of poltergeist activity is the Enfield Poltergeist in London, which took place in the late 1970s. This case involved a family living in a modest council house in the London borough of Enfield. The family, consisting of a single mother, Peggy Hodgson, and her four children, began experiencing a series of increasingly disturbing events that drew the attention of the media, paranormal investigators, and skeptics alike.

The activity began in August 1977, when Peggy Hodgson reported that furniture in her daughters' bedroom was moving on its own. This initial incident was followed by a series of loud knocking sounds, disembodied voices, and the unexplained movement of objects throughout the house. The events seemed to center around the two Hodgson daughters, Janet and Margaret, particularly the younger Janet, who was 11 years old at the time.

Over the next 18 months, the family reported a wide range of phenomena, including toys and other household items being thrown across rooms, strange noises, and even sightings of apparitions. The activity was witnessed by multiple people, including neighbors, police officers, and reporters, who all attested to the strange occurrences. The case gained widespread attention, with newspapers and television programs covering the ongoing disturbances.

One of the most chilling aspects of the Enfield Poltergeist was the emergence of a deep, gravelly voice that seemed to come from Janet herself. This voice, which purported to be that of a deceased man named Bill Wilkins, would speak through Janet, often in a threatening or mocking tone. Skeptics argued that Janet was faking the voice, but tests conducted by investigators, such as taping Janet's mouth shut while the voice continued, suggested that something more unusual might be occurring.

Paranormal investigators from the Society for Psychical Research, including Maurice Grosse and Guy Lyon Playfair, spent extended periods at the Hodgson house, documenting the phenomena and interviewing witnesses. While some skeptics dismissed the case as a hoax, Grosse and Playfair were convinced that the events were genuine, citing the sheer number of witnesses and the consistency of the reports.

The Enfield Poltergeist case remains one of the most compelling examples of poltergeist activity, with many of the phenomena fitting the classic profile of a poltergeist haunting: physical disturbances, strange noises, and a focus on a particular individual, in this case, young Janet Hodgson.

Historical and Modern Cases
Poltergeist activity is not a phenomenon confined to modern times; it has been reported throughout history and across cultures. Historical accounts of poltergeists often describe very similar phenomena to those reported in contemporary cases, suggesting that this type of haunting is a persistent and widespread occurrence.

One of the earliest recorded cases of poltergeist activity dates back to the 17th century in England, known as the Drummer of Tedworth. In 1661, John Mompesson, a landowner in Tedworth (now Tidworth), Wiltshire, confiscated a drum from a local drummer named William Drury, who was accused of collecting money under false pretenses. Shortly after, Mompesson's house became the site of strange disturbances, including the sound of drumming, knocking, and objects being thrown around by an unseen force. The activity was attributed to Drury's supposed magical abilities or a curse placed upon the house, and it continued for several months before gradually fading away.

In more recent times, the Bell Witch case from Tennessee in the early 19th century has become one of the most famous poltergeist cases in American history. The Bell family reported being tormented by an unseen entity that was capable of speech, physical attacks, and even appearing as a spectral figure. The disturbances, which began in 1817, included knocking on the walls, physical assaults on the family members, and strange, disembodied voices that identified themselves as the "Witch" of Kate Batts, a neighbor with whom the Bell family had disputes.

The Bell Witch case remains one of the most extensively documented cases of poltergeist activity in the United States.

Case Studies and Eyewitness Accounts
Eyewitness accounts are crucial in poltergeist investigations because the phenomena are often difficult to document scientifically due to their sporadic and unpredictable nature. Case studies involving multiple, credible witnesses who provide consistent reports of their experiences can be particularly compelling.

For example, in the case of the Rosenheim Poltergeist in Germany in 1967, the activity occurred in the law office of Sigmund Adam. The disturbances included phones ringing without being connected, lights flickering, and office furniture moving on its own. The events were witnessed by multiple employees, clients, and even police officers, making it one of the most well-documented poltergeist cases. Investigators, including physicist Dr. Friedbert Karger, conducted extensive studies, yet could not find a conventional explanation for the phenomena, leading some to consider psychokinesis as a possible cause.

Eyewitness accounts from these cases often describe the fear and confusion experienced by those involved. For the witnesses, poltergeist activity is not merely a theoretical or abstract phenomenon but a deeply personal and often traumatic experience. The consistency of reports across different cases and cultures adds weight to the argument that poltergeists represent a genuine, if not fully understood, aspect of the paranormal.

Importance of Modern Investigations and Eyewitness Accounts in Building Evidence

Modern investigations into poltergeist activity often rely heavily on eyewitness accounts, as well as the use of technology to capture evidence of the disturbances. While capturing definitive proof of poltergeist phenomena remains challenging, advances in audio and video recording, as well as environmental monitoring equipment, have provided investigators with more tools to document these events.

The value of eyewitness accounts cannot be overstated. In many cases, the sheer number of witnesses, their credibility, and the consistency of their reports provide compelling evidence that something extraordinary is happening. These accounts are often supported by physical evidence, such as objects being moved or damaged, which can be examined and analyzed.

Furthermore, modern investigations often involve a multidisciplinary approach, incorporating perspectives from psychology, physics, and parapsychology to explore the potential causes of poltergeist phenomena. By combining rigorous investigation

CONCLUSION

In this chapter, we have explored the various types of ghostly phenomena that have been reported throughout history, including residual ghosts, intelligent spirits, and poltergeists. These accounts, which span across cultures and centuries, consistently point to the existence of a mechanism by which energy, whether residual or intelligent, appears to be preserved after death. The energy of a Roman soldier replaying in a cellar, or the conscious presence of an intelligent spirit interacting with the living, suggests that some aspect of human existence may persist beyond physical demise.

What these reports collectively indicate is that there is a compelling case to be made for the survival of energy or consciousness after death. Whether it is the repetitive, non-interactive replay of a past event or the deliberate actions of an intelligent spirit, these phenomena suggest that something of the human experience continues to exist and manifest in the physical world, even after the body has ceased to function.

While we may not yet fully understand the precise mechanisms by which these ghosts occur, the sheer volume of evidence—documented cases, eyewitness accounts, and historical records—makes it increasingly difficult to dismiss these phenomena as mere superstition or psychological aberrations. The consistency and persistence of these reports suggest that ghosts, in their various forms, are a real phenomenon that merits serious consideration.

In conclusion, the evidence we have examined in this chapter strongly supports the notion that some form of energy or consciousness survives death. This realization challenges our understanding of life and death, opening the door to new possibilities about the nature of existence and the potential for life beyond the grave. As we continue to investigate and explore these mysterious phenomena, it is crucial to keep an open mind and acknowledge that the presence of ghosts—whether residual, intelligent, or otherwise—may provide a window into the enduring mysteries of consciousness and the afterlife.

In the search for evidence of the afterlife, paranormal researchers have long sought to gather and analyze data that goes beyond the anecdotal. To build a compelling case for the existence of ghosts, it is essential to draw upon a diverse array of evidence, each piece contributing to a more complete picture of the paranormal. Among the most intriguing sources of such evidence are Electronic Voice Phenomena (EVP) and the unexpected detections made by advanced technological sensors, such as those found in Tesla vehicles. These sources, when considered together, offer a tantalizing glimpse into a world that remains hidden from our everyday senses but may be revealed through the right tools and techniques.

The Evidence from EVP: Voices from Beyond

EVP has long held a significant place in paranormal investigation, providing what many believe to be direct communication from spirits. These phenomena are typically captured on audio recordings, where voices or sounds, not heard at the time of recording, are discovered upon playback. The nature of EVP has sparked considerable debate, with skeptics attributing these sounds to audio pareidolia (the tendency of the brain to find patterns in random data), electromagnetic interference, or even intentional hoaxes. However, the consistency and specificity of certain EVP recordings suggest that there might be more to these phenomena than simple misinterpretation.

Clear, Intelligible Phrases or Responses

In many instances, EVPs have captured distinct voices answering direct questions posed by investigators. These responses often display contextually appropriate language, tone, and inflection—characteristics that are challenging to dismiss as random noise.

For example, in the famously haunted Eastern State Penitentiary in Philadelphia, investigators have repeatedly captured a deep, gravelly voice responding to questions about the prison's notorious past. One particular session recorded an EVP where the voice unmistakably muttered, "I'm still here," in response to a question about whether any spirits remained. The specificity of the language and the emotion conveyed in the voice suggest a conscious entity attempting to communicate.

Multiple Independent Recordings at the Same Location

In locations with a history of paranormal activity, different investigators have independently captured similar voices or messages, adding weight to the argument that something genuine is being recorded.

The Queen Mary, a retired ocean liner now permanently docked in Long Beach, California, is renowned for its paranormal activity. Various paranormal teams have captured EVPs in the ship's pool area, where a little girl's voice repeatedly calls out for her mother. These recordings have been made years apart by different teams, yet the voice remains consistent in tone and content, leading many to believe that the same spirit is attempting to communicate.

EVPs with Verifiable Information

Perhaps the most striking are those EVPs that provide information unknown to the researchers at the time but later verified as accurate. These instances challenge the notion that such phenomena can be purely coincidental or fabricated.

In one well-documented case from the Myrtles Plantation in Louisiana, investigators recorded an EVP that mentioned a specific name—"Chloe." This name was unfamiliar to the team, but later research revealed that Chloe was indeed a former slave on the plantation, who, according to legend, had been involved in a tragic poisoning incident. The fact that the name was unknown to the researchers at the time lends credence to the idea that they had captured a genuine spirit communication.

The Evidence from Advanced Technology: Unseen Entities Revealed

In recent years, technology has advanced to the point where devices are capable of detecting phenomena beyond the range of human senses. This has led to intriguing reports of unexplained detections, particularly from the sophisticated sensors used in Tesla vehicles. These technologies, designed to enhance safety and navigation, have sometimes recorded inexplicable figures or triggered alerts in the absence of any visible cause.

Tesla's Autopilot System Reacting to Unseen Figures

There have been multiple accounts of Tesla vehicles detecting "persons" on dark roads or near cemeteries, where no one was visibly present. These detections have sometimes led the vehicle to take evasive actions, as if avoiding an obstacle that the driver could not see.

One striking example occurred near Bachelor's Grove Cemetery, a notoriously haunted location in Illinois. A Tesla driving past the cemetery at night detected a figure standing by the side of the road. The car's autopilot system initiated a braking maneuver, even though the driver saw nothing. Later review of the car's sensor data showed an outline of what appeared to be a person, yet no one was there. The incident raises questions about whether the vehicle's sensors are picking up on energies or entities that are invisible to the human eye.

Dashboard Cameras Capturing Translucent Figures

On occasion, dashboard cameras have recorded what appear to be humanoid shapes, often faint and translucent, triggering the car's collision warnings. These incidents suggest that the sensors are picking up something that does not register on the visible spectrum.

A video from a driver in Japan captures such an event. As the car moves through a deserted road at night, the dashboard camera clearly shows a faint, ghostly figure crossing the road, triggering the collision alert. The figure is not visible to the naked eye, but the camera and sensors both registered its presence. This footage has been widely discussed in paranormal circles as potential evidence of a spirit caught on modern technology.

Infrared Cameras Revealing Strange Energy Patterns

In paranormal investigations, infrared cameras have detected anomalous heat signatures or energy patterns that coincide with reports of apparitions. These patterns often align with the locations of reported sightings, suggesting a correlation between the technology's readings and the phenomena.

One famous case comes from the Stanley Hotel in Colorado, the inspiration for Stephen King's *The Shining*. During an investigation, infrared cameras captured a distinct, human-shaped heat signature in an otherwise empty hallway. This occurred simultaneously with reports from guests and staff of seeing a shadowy figure in the same area. The alignment of these different forms of evidence—eyewitness accounts, infrared detection, and the historical reputation of the location—strongly suggests the presence of a paranormal entity.

Connecting the Dots: A Holistic Approach to Paranormal Evidence

When analyzed together, the evidence from EVP and advanced technology can offer mutual reinforcement, each lending credibility to the other. If these two distinct methods are capturing similar anomalies in the same locations, it strengthens the argument that they are both detecting aspects of the same underlying phenomena.

For instance, if a Tesla's sensors detect a mysterious figure in a location previously known for capturing EVPs, this cross-verification could indicate that both technologies are interacting with the same entity or energy. Similarly, an EVP that describes the appearance of an apparition, which is later confirmed by a visual detection on advanced sensors, would provide a powerful link between auditory and visual paranormal evidence.

Consider the case of Waverly Hills Sanatorium in Kentucky, one of the most haunted locations in the United States. EVPs recorded here have consistently mentioned a shadowy figure known as the "Creeper," often described as crawling along walls or ceilings. When paranormal teams introduced advanced infrared and motion-sensing technology, these devices recorded anomalous movements that matched the descriptions given in the EVPs. This correlation between audio and visual data strengthens the argument that the phenomena experienced at Waverly Hills are not merely figments of imagination but represent genuine interactions with the paranormal.

Conclusion: A New Era of Paranormal Investigation

The intersection of traditional paranormal investigation techniques, like EVP, with cutting-edge technology opens new avenues for exploring and understanding the mysteries of the afterlife. By combining these methods, researchers can build a more robust and compelling case for the existence of ghosts, one that is harder to dismiss with conventional skepticism.

The evidence from EVP and advanced technological sensors, when carefully collected and analyzed, offers a glimpse into a reality that lies just beyond our ordinary perception. While this evidence may not satisfy every skeptic, it provides a compelling argument for those open to the possibility that our world is more complex and mysterious than we often assume. By continuing to refine these methods and exploring new technologies, we move closer to answering the age-old question of whether ghosts truly exist and, by extension, what awaits us after death.

THE NON-LOCAL MIND: EXPLORING ESP AND TELEPATHY

Throughout the history of consciousness research, phenomena like Extrasensory Perception (ESP) and telepathy have intrigued scientists, philosophers, and parapsychologists alike. These phenomena challenge conventional materialist views of the brain, suggesting that consciousness might possess non-local properties—that is, the ability to perceive or interact with information beyond the constraints of space and time. One institution that has contributed significantly to the study of these ideas is the Rhine Research Center (formerly the Duke Parapsychology Laboratory), which has provided statistical evidence supporting the existence of telepathy and other forms of ESP.

This chapter will explore the findings from studies conducted by the Rhine Institute and other research centers on telepathy, highlighting how these experiments offer statistical support for the notion that the mind may operate in ways that transcend conventional physical boundaries. By examining the scientific basis for ESP, we will consider how this evidence suggests the brain might be capable of perceiving information in a non-local manner, reshaping our understanding of consciousness.

THE RHINE INSTITUTE AND THE STUDY OF ESP

The Rhine Research Center, founded by Dr. J.B. Rhine at Duke University in the 1930s, became one of the world's leading centers for the scientific investigation of ESP, including telepathy, clairvoyance, precognition, and psychokinesis. Rhine's early work set the foundation for modern parapsychology, emphasizing the need for controlled, empirical studies to determine whether human consciousness could access information beyond the limits of ordinary sensory perception.

The most iconic studies conducted by Rhine involved the use of **Zener cards**—a deck of 25 cards featuring five distinct symbols. Subjects were tasked with guessing the symbols on the cards without seeing them, either in a telepathic experiment (where another person viewed the cards) or in a clairvoyant setting (where no one viewed the cards). Over tens of thousands of trials, Rhine observed results that appeared to deviate significantly from chance, suggesting the presence of a genuine telepathic or clairvoyant ability. These findings became a cornerstone for claims of statistical evidence for ESP, with researchers continuing to build on Rhine's work in the decades that followed.

Statistical Evidence for Telepathy

One of the critical achievements of Rhine's research was the application of **statistical methods** to parapsychology, allowing researchers to rigorously evaluate the results of telepathy and ESP experiments. By calculating the odds of participants guessing symbols correctly by chance, Rhine demonstrated that certain individuals consistently achieved higher-than-expected success rates. In some studies, the probability of obtaining such results by chance was calculated to be **one in several million**, lending credence to the hypothesis that telepathic or extrasensory abilities might indeed exist.

These studies provided a wealth of data that pointed to the possibility of **non-local perception**—the idea that information can be accessed without physical proximity or sensory input. The implications of such findings are profound. If consciousness can access information at a distance, it challenges the classical view that the brain is confined to processing information received through the senses or the immediate environment. Telepathy, as evidenced in Rhine's experiments, suggests that consciousness may operate in ways that are untethered to the usual spatial and temporal limitations imposed by the physical brain.

BEYOND RHINE: MODERN PARAPSYCHOLOGICAL STUDIES

Following Rhine's pioneering work, many other researchers and institutions expanded on the study of ESP and telepathy. **Ganzfeld experiments** became a notable method used to investigate telepathy in a more controlled environment. In these experiments, one participant (the "receiver") was placed in a sensory-deprivation state, while another participant (the "sender") viewed images or scenes in a separate location. The receiver then attempted to describe the image or scene being sent to them.

Meta-analyses of Ganzfeld studies have shown consistent, though often modest, results that are statistically significant. In some cases, these results indicate that the odds of participants correctly identifying the target images by chance alone are exceedingly small. The findings from these experiments further support the notion that telepathy or some form of non-local information transfer may be occurring, with the brain acting as a receiver of distant signals or information.

Remote viewing is another area of research that supports the idea of non-local perception. Remote viewing involves participants describing a distant location or object that they cannot physically perceive. Studies conducted by researchers at institutions like the Stanford Research Institute (SRI) yielded surprising results, with participants often able to describe distant locations with remarkable accuracy. The consistency of these results across various studies adds weight to the theory that consciousness can access information from afar, without reliance on physical proximity.

THE QUANTUM BRAIN

While the statistical evidence for telepathy and non-local perception is compelling, it raises important questions about how the brain or consciousness could achieve such feats. Traditional neuroscience, which views the brain as a biological processor confined to local sensory input, struggles to explain these findings. However, emerging theories from **quantum physics** offer intriguing possibilities.

Some theorists, such as **Roger Penrose** and **Stuart Hameroff**, suggest that consciousness may involve quantum processes within the brain. Their **Orchestrated Objective Reduction (Orch-OR) theory** proposes that microtubules within neurons could operate at the quantum level, enabling the brain to interact with non-local information in ways akin to quantum entanglement. In quantum entanglement, particles remain instantaneously connected regardless of distance, defying classical notions of space and time. If similar quantum mechanisms are at play within the brain, they could provide a plausible explanation for telepathy and other forms of ESP.

While the **Orch-OR theory** remains speculative, it aligns with the statistical evidence from parapsychological research, suggesting that consciousness may be capable of accessing information beyond the limitations of space and time. This quantum perspective could help explain how the brain engages in non-local perception and why telepathy appears to function in a manner that is not bound by physical proximity.

Implications for Consciousness and the Nature of Reality

The evidence for ESP and telepathy, particularly the statistical data from institutions like the Rhine Research Center, challenges conventional understandings of the brain and consciousness. If consciousness can indeed access information remotely, it suggests that the mind operates on principles that are not fully captured by our current scientific paradigms.

This opens the door to a new understanding of **consciousness as a non-local phenomenon**—a view that could reshape our perceptions of the brain, mind, and reality itself. Telepathy and similar phenomena imply that consciousness might not be a byproduct of localized neural activity, but rather a more expansive and interconnected field that transcends individual brains. This would have profound implications for fields ranging from neuroscience and psychology to physics and philosophy.

Conclusion: Telepathy as Evidence for the Non-Local Mind

The statistical evidence for telepathy and ESP, as provided by the Rhine Research Center and later experiments, points to the possibility that the brain can perceive information in a non-local way. The ability of individuals to consistently perform beyond chance in controlled experiments suggests that consciousness may operate beyond the constraints of space and time. Whether through quantum processes or as part of an unknown mechanism, the existence of telepathy challenges the materialistic view of the brain and invites us to consider that consciousness may be more far-reaching than we ever imagined.

As research into ESP and telepathy continues, we are compelled to rethink the boundaries of consciousness and its relationship to the physical world. The data gathered from these studies provide not only statistical evidence but also a philosophical and scientific invitation to explore the strange, non-local nature of the mind.

MEDIUMS

INTRODUCTION

Mediumship, the practice of communicating with the spirits of the deceased, has been a part of human culture for centuries. From ancient shamans to modern-day psychics, the ability to convey messages from the dead has fascinated, comforted, and, at times, terrified the living. Central to the concept of mediumship is the belief that consciousness persists beyond death and that it is possible for the living to receive information from those who have passed on. This chapter explores the phenomenon of mediumship through a discussion of some of the most compelling and well-documented cases, where mediums have provided information that was known only to the deceased, often with startling accuracy.

These cases are supported by interviews, testimonies, and detailed records, offering a compelling argument that mediumship may serve as a genuine means of communication with the afterlife. By examining these instances, we can begin to assess the potential mechanisms of information transmission between the living and the dead, and what these phenomena might suggest about the nature of consciousness and life after death.

THE CASE OF LEONORA PIPER

One of the most famous and extensively studied mediums in history is Leonora Piper, a Boston-based medium whose abilities were investigated by some of the most prominent researchers of her time. Born in 1857, Piper's reputation as a medium began to grow in the 1880s when she started holding séances that attracted the attention of scholars and scientists.

Dr. Richard Hodgson, a member of the Society for Psychical Research (SPR), conducted an in-depth investigation of Piper's abilities over a period of nearly two decades. Hodgson, who initially approached the study with skepticism, became convinced of her genuine abilities after witnessing her provide information that seemed impossible to obtain through ordinary means. Piper, during her trances, would channel various personalities who claimed to be deceased individuals. These personalities would provide detailed information about their lives, often including facts that were unknown to the sitters and were later verified as accurate.

One of the most compelling aspects of Piper's mediumship was her ability to provide information that was not only accurate but also highly specific. For instance, during one of her séances, Piper channeled a spirit who identified himself as George Pelham, a deceased friend of one of Hodgson's colleagues. The spirit provided intricate details about Pelham's life, including personal memories and relationships, that were later confirmed by the colleague. What made this case particularly remarkable was the consistency of the information provided across multiple séances, even when different sitters were involved. Pelham's spirit would recognize and address people he knew in life, offering personalized messages that were deeply meaningful to those present.

The case of Leonora Piper stands out not only because of the accuracy of the information she provided but also due to the rigorous scientific scrutiny under which she was studied. Researchers like Hodgson and William James, a prominent psychologist and philosopher, were unable to find any evidence of fraud or deception, leading them to conclude that Piper's mediumship was a genuine phenomenon that merited serious consideration.

THE CROSS-CORRESPONDENCES

Another significant set of mediumship cases that has intrigued researchers for over a century is the Cross-Correspondences. These cases involve a group of mediums, primarily in the United Kingdom, who, over the course of several years, received fragmented messages that only made sense when combined with messages received by other mediums. The Cross-Correspondences were orchestrated by a group of deceased members of the Society for Psychical Research, including Frederic W. H. Myers, who, during their lifetimes, had been deeply involved in the study of psychical phenomena.

The messages received by the mediums were often cryptic and complex, involving references to classical literature, poetry, and philosophical ideas. These references were carefully chosen and distributed across different mediums, making it nearly impossible for any single medium to understand the full message independently. The intention seemed to be to create a "cross-correspondence" that would serve as proof of survival after death, demonstrating that the deceased were working together to communicate a coherent message.

One of the most famous cross-correspondences involved the phrase "Let us cross the Styx together," which appeared in the messages received by different mediums. This phrase was a reference to the River Styx in Greek mythology, which souls must cross to enter the afterlife. The phrase, along with other interconnected messages, only made sense when researchers from the SPR compared the transcripts from multiple mediums and pieced together the full meaning.

The Cross-Correspondences were so intricate and involved that they became a central focus of the SPR's research for decades. The sheer complexity and the apparent need for coordination among the deceased communicators suggest a deliberate attempt to provide compelling evidence of life after death. Critics have argued that the cases could be explained by unconscious telepathy among the mediums, but the level of detail and the specific literary knowledge required to create the correspondences make this explanation less plausible.

THE RUDI SCHNEIDER CASE

Rudi Schneider, an Austrian medium, was known for his physical mediumship, where spirits allegedly interacted with the physical environment, producing tangible phenomena such as moving objects, cold breezes, and the appearance of ectoplasm. Schneider's séances were attended by numerous researchers, including Dr. Harry Price, a well-known paranormal investigator, who meticulously documented the events.

One of the most compelling aspects of Schneider's mediumship was the apparent interaction between the spirits and the physical environment. In controlled settings, objects would move without any visible means of manipulation, and lights would flicker or extinguish entirely. What made Schneider's case particularly significant was the level of control exerted by the investigators. Séances were often conducted under strict conditions to prevent fraud, including the use of infrared cameras and other devices to detect any tampering. Despite these measures, the phenomena continued to occur, leading some researchers to conclude that Schneider was genuinely in contact with the spirit world.

In one particularly notable séance, Schneider, under strict supervision, produced a series of levitations and object movements that were captured on film. The objects moved in ways that defied conventional explanation, such as a table rising several inches off the ground without any apparent force acting upon it. The investigators, who included skeptics as well as believers, were unable to find any evidence of trickery, further supporting the authenticity of the phenomena.

Schneider's mediumship provided not only evidence of communication with the deceased but also raised questions about the potential for the spirit world to influence the physical environment. While the exact mechanisms behind these phenomena remain unknown, the documented events suggest that mediumship might involve more than just information transmission—it could also entail a direct interaction between the living and the spirit world.

THE CASE OF CHICO XAVIER

Chico Xavier, one of Brazil's most famous mediums, authored over 400 books that he claimed were dictated to him by spirits. His work was widely recognized not only for its spiritual content but also for the detailed and accurate information it often contained, much of which was unknown to Xavier before he wrote it.

One of the most compelling cases involving Xavier was the so-called "Letters from the Dead." In these letters, Xavier claimed to channel messages from deceased individuals to their living relatives. These messages often contained highly specific details about the deceased's life, including personal information that was not publicly known. In some cases, the letters even provided information that helped solve legal disputes, such as the rightful heir in inheritance cases.

A particularly striking example involved a letter from a deceased young man named José. In the letter, which was addressed to his mother, José provided detailed descriptions of his death, including the precise location where he had been shot and the circumstances leading up to the event. The accuracy of the information was later confirmed by the police investigation, which matched José's account with the evidence found at the crime scene. José's mother, who had been struggling to come to terms with her son's death, found solace in the letter, which not only provided closure but also contained details that were unknown to anyone but the deceased and the investigators.

Chico Xavier's mediumship was not only significant for its volume but also for the impact it had on the lives of those who received messages from their deceased loved ones. The accuracy of the information provided, often verified by independent sources, made Xavier one of the most respected and credible mediums of the 20th century.

CONCLUSION

The phenomena associated with mediumship present a significant challenge to conventional understandings of consciousness and reality. While skeptics often dismiss mediums as con artists or fantasists, the cases explored in this chapter provide compelling evidence that cannot be easily explained away. Mediums like Leonora Piper, who was subjected to rigorous scientific scrutiny, and the complex Cross-Correspondences offer a strong foundation for considering mediumship as a genuine means of communication with the deceased. The physical phenomena associated with Rudi Schneider and the detailed, verifiable messages channeled by Chico Xavier further bolster the argument that mediums may indeed access information from 'beyond.'

These cases suggest that consciousness may not only persist after death but also retain the ability to interact with and transmit information to the living. This challenges the materialistic view that consciousness is merely a byproduct of brain activity, confined to the physical body. Instead, it opens the possibility that the mind or spirit continues to exist independently, with the capacity to reach out to the world of the living.

The consistency, accuracy, and specificity of the information provided by these mediums, often verified under controlled conditions, cannot be dismissed as mere coincidence or fraud. These accounts force us to reconsider our assumptions about the nature of reality and the boundaries of human experience. They hint at the existence of other realms or dimensions—places where consciousness might reside after death and from which it can communicate with those still living.

As we delve deeper into the mysteries of consciousness and the afterlife throughout this book, it becomes increasingly clear that mediumship may be more than just a curious phenomenon; it could be a crucial key to understanding the true nature of existence. The idea that life after death is not just a comforting belief but a reality grounded in evidence deserves serious consideration. Mediumship, with its potential to bridge the gap between the living and the deceased, offers a powerful and intriguing window into realms that are still largely unexplored by science.

In embracing this possibility, we are invited to expand our understanding of what it means to be alive, to be conscious, and to persist beyond the physical realm. The evidence gathered in this exploration suggests that the afterlife is not merely a matter of faith, but a domain that can be approached with reason, inquiry, and a willingness to explore the unknown. Mediumship, when rigorously examined, may indeed reveal that the boundaries between life and death are far more porous than we have ever imagined, pointing to a continuity of existence that transcends our current understanding of reality.

DEATHBED AND CRISIS APPARITIONS

Introduction

Among the many forms of paranormal phenomena, deathbed and crisis apparitions hold a unique place due to their intimate connection with the moments surrounding death or extreme peril. These apparitions typically involve the appearance of deceased loved ones or other figures who seem to provide comfort, guidance, or warnings to those on the brink of death or in life-threatening situations. Such experiences are reported across cultures and time periods, often described as deeply emotional and transformative for those who experience them.

In this chapter, we will explore the nature of deathbed and crisis apparitions, examining their possible significance within the broader framework of consciousness and life after death. By delving into well-documented cases, such as the apparitions associated with the tragic crash of Eastern Air Lines Flight 401, we will consider how these phenomena might provide evidence for the persistence of consciousness beyond the physical body. The recurring themes and patterns in these accounts suggest that they may not merely be hallucinations or figments of a stressed mind, but rather meaningful encounters that hint at a reality beyond our current understanding.

What Are Deathbed and Crisis Apparitions?

Deathbed apparitions, often referred to as deathbed visions, typically occur in the final moments of a person's life. These experiences involve the dying individual seeing or interacting with deceased loved ones, religious figures, or other comforting presences. These apparitions are often perceived as coming to assist the person in transitioning from life to death, offering reassurance and peace in their final moments.

Crisis apparitions, on the other hand, occur during moments of extreme distress, danger, or imminent death. These apparitions can appear to individuals who are not necessarily dying but are facing a critical situation, such as a severe illness, an accident, or a near-death experience. Like deathbed apparitions, crisis apparitions often involve the appearance of deceased loved ones or other familiar figures, providing comfort or guidance during the crisis.

What distinguishes these apparitions from other types of ghostly encounters is their timing and emotional impact. They tend to occur spontaneously and are often accompanied by a sense of calm or acceptance, even in the face of impending death. The significance of these experiences lies not only in their immediate emotional effects but also in the broader implications they hold for our understanding of consciousness and the afterlife.

CASE STUDY: THE GHOSTS OF FLIGHT 401

One of the most compelling examples of crisis apparitions involves the case of Eastern Air Lines Flight 401, which crashed into the Florida Everglades on December 29, 1972. The flight was en route from New York City to Miami when a series of technical malfunctions and pilot errors led to the tragic crash, resulting in the deaths of 101 of the 176 people on board, including Captain Robert Loft and Flight Engineer Donald Repo.

In the months and years following the crash, numerous reports emerged from Eastern Air Lines employees, particularly those working on other L-1011 aircraft, who claimed to have encountered apparitions of Captain Loft and Engineer Repo. These apparitions were reported not only by flight attendants and pilots but also by passengers. The sightings were often associated with warnings of potential mechanical failures or other dangers, which, when heeded, seemed to prevent further disasters.

One of the most notable accounts came from a flight attendant who reported seeing Captain Loft's apparition sitting in the cockpit of an aircraft that had been fitted with salvaged parts from Flight 401. She claimed that the figure of Loft told her to check the aircraft's systems, which led to the discovery of a serious issue that could have caused another crash. Similar stories involved Engineer Repo appearing to mechanics and other crew members, urging them to repair specific components before takeoff.

These reports were so frequent and consistent that they became part of the airline's lore, leading to an investigation by Eastern Air Lines. Although the company officially dismissed the stories as rumors, many employees believed that the spirits of Loft and Repo were genuinely trying to prevent further tragedies. The apparitions ceased once the airline reportedly removed all salvaged parts from other aircraft.

The Ghosts of Flight 401 case is significant not only for the number of credible witnesses but also for the nature of the apparitions themselves. These were not random sightings but rather purposeful interactions that appeared to serve a protective function. The consistency of the reports, combined with the specific details provided by the apparitions, suggests that these were not mere hallucinations but potentially genuine crisis apparitions with a clear intent to communicate and prevent further loss of life.

OTHER EXAMPLES OF DEATHBED AND CRISIS APPARITIONS

The Ghosts of Flight 401 is just one of many documented cases of crisis apparitions. Another well-known example involves the Titanic disaster in 1912. There are numerous reports from survivors who claimed to have seen deceased loved ones or other comforting figures during the harrowing hours after the ship struck an iceberg and began to sink. These apparitions were often described as providing reassurance or guiding the survivors toward safety.

Similarly, during the First World War, there were widespread reports of soldiers experiencing crisis apparitions on the battlefield. In some instances, soldiers claimed to see visions of their deceased comrades or family members just before they themselves were wounded or killed. These apparitions were often interpreted as harbingers of death or as comforting presences meant to ease the transition from life to death.

Deathbed apparitions are also widely reported in hospice settings, where patients nearing the end of their lives often speak of seeing deceased loved ones or spiritual beings. These visions are typically described as peaceful and comforting, with the dying person expressing a sense of readiness to move on. In many cases, these experiences are witnessed by family members or healthcare providers, adding to their credibility.

One particularly compelling case involved Sir William Barrett, a professor of physics, who documented his wife's experience with a dying patient who had a vivid deathbed vision. The patient, a young woman, spoke of seeing her deceased father, who had come to take her with him. As she described this vision, her face lit up with joy and serenity. What made this case especially noteworthy was that the woman also mentioned seeing her recently deceased sister, news of whose death had been deliberately withheld from her to avoid distress. This detail, unknown to the patient, strongly suggests that her vision was not a mere hallucination but a genuine encounter with the deceased.

SIGNIFICANCE OF DEATHBED AND CRISIS APPARITIONS

The significance of deathbed and crisis apparitions lies in their potential implications for our understanding of consciousness and the afterlife. These experiences suggest that consciousness may not be confined to the physical body and could persist beyond death. The consistent themes of comfort, guidance, and reassurance in these apparitions indicate that they may serve a purpose in helping individuals transition from life to death or in protecting them during moments of extreme peril.

From a psychological perspective, some researchers argue that these apparitions could be the mind's way of coping with the stress of impending death or danger. However, the specific details and accuracy of the information provided by these apparitions often go beyond what could be expected from a purely psychological or hallucinatory experience. The fact that these experiences are reported across cultures and historical periods, with remarkable consistency, adds weight to the argument that they may represent genuine encounters with the afterlife.

Moreover, the impact of these apparitions on those who experience them cannot be understated. For many, these visions provide comfort and a sense of peace in their final moments, easing the fear of death and offering hope of a continued existence beyond the physical realm. For others, particularly those who encounter crisis apparitions, the experiences can be life-saving, as in the case of the Ghosts of Flight 401.

Conclusion

In exploring deathbed and crisis apparitions, we encounter phenomena that challenge our understanding of life, death, and the nature of consciousness. These apparitions, whether they occur at the moment of death or during times of extreme crisis, consistently suggest that consciousness may persist beyond the physical body and that there may be a form of existence after death.

The cases discussed in this chapter, including the Ghosts of Flight 401 and other well-documented examples, provide compelling evidence that these experiences are more than just hallucinations or psychological phenomena. Instead, they may represent genuine interactions with the deceased, offering comfort, guidance, and protection in moments of profound significance.

As we continue to study and document these phenomena, deathbed and crisis apparitions offer a unique and powerful window into the mysteries of consciousness and the possibility of life after death. These experiences not only provide solace to those facing death but also challenge us to broaden our understanding of what it means to live and to die, suggesting that the journey of consciousness may continue long after the physical body has ceased to function.

REINCARNATION

EXPLANATION OF THE CONCEPT OF REINCARNATION

Reincarnation, the belief that the soul or consciousness can be reborn into a new body after death, is one of the most enduring and widely held spiritual concepts across human history. This idea posits that life is not a singular, linear experience but rather a cycle of birth, death, and rebirth, where each life offers the soul opportunities for growth, learning, and evolution. The notion of reincarnation suggests that our current existence is just one of many, with past lives influencing our present and future lives shaped by the choices we make in this one.

At its core, reincarnation hinges on the belief that the soul is immortal, surviving the death of the physical body and moving on to inhabit a new one. This process is often seen as a means of spiritual progression, where each life serves as a lesson or a step in the soul's journey toward greater understanding, enlightenment, or fulfillment. The circumstances of each reincarnation—such as the environment, relationships, challenges, and opportunities—are believed to be influenced by the actions and decisions of previous lives, a concept often referred to as karma.

Karma, a central tenet in many reincarnation-believing cultures, operates on the principle of cause and effect. It suggests that the actions, thoughts, and intentions from one life impact future lives, creating a moral framework within which the soul's journey unfolds. Positive actions and growth in one life lead to favorable conditions in the next, while unresolved issues or negative behaviors may result in challenges that the soul must face in subsequent incarnations.

Reincarnation is more than just a spiritual or religious belief; it also offers a framework for understanding human experiences, relationships, and the trials and tribulations of life. It suggests that the pains and joys of life are not random but are tied to a broader, ongoing journey that transcends a single lifetime. This perspective provides comfort to many, offering a sense of continuity and purpose beyond the confines of our current existence.

Reincarnation in Various Cultures and Religions

Reincarnation is a concept that spans numerous cultures and religions, each with its own interpretation and nuances. Perhaps the most well-known traditions that incorporate reincarnation are Hinduism, Buddhism, Jainism, and certain forms of New Age spirituality, but the belief in rebirth can also be found in other religious and cultural contexts around the world.

Hinduism is perhaps the most well-known religion where reincarnation is a central doctrine. In Hindu thought, the cycle of birth, death, and rebirth is known as samsara. The ultimate goal for the soul, or atman, is to achieve moksha, or liberation from the cycle of samsara. This liberation is achieved through spiritual growth, adherence to dharma (righteous duty), and the accumulation of good karma across many lifetimes. The Bhagavad Gita, one of Hinduism's most sacred texts, elaborates on the nature of the soul, describing it as eternal and indestructible, merely passing from one body to another like a person changing clothes.

Buddhism shares the concept of samsara but places a different emphasis on the nature of the self. Unlike Hinduism, which believes in a permanent soul, Buddhism teaches the doctrine of anatta, or no-self, where what is reborn is not a fixed soul but a stream of consciousness or karmic energy. This energy, shaped by one's actions, thoughts, and desires, continues into a new life, perpetuating the cycle of birth, death, and rebirth. The ultimate goal in Buddhism is to achieve nirvana, a state of liberation where one is freed from the cycle of samsara by overcoming desire and ignorance.

Jainism also believes in the cycle of reincarnation, emphasizing the importance of non-violence (ahimsa) and the accumulation of positive karma to achieve liberation. In Jainism, the soul is seen as inherently pure, but it is weighed down by karmic particles that result from actions and desires. Through strict ethical conduct, meditation, and renunciation, a soul can purify itself and eventually attain kevala, or omniscience, leading to liberation from the cycle of rebirth.

In addition to these Eastern religions, New Age spiritual movements have adopted and adapted the concept of reincarnation, often blending it with ideas from Western esotericism, astrology, and other spiritual practices. In these contexts, reincarnation is frequently discussed in terms of soul lessons, spiritual contracts, and life missions. The idea of past-life regression therapy, where individuals are guided to recall previous lives to heal present-life issues, has also become popular within these movements.

Interestingly, belief in reincarnation is not limited to Eastern religions and New Age thought. Ancient Greek philosophy also entertained the idea of the transmigration of souls. Philosophers like Pythagoras and Plato believed in the immortality of the soul and its journey through various incarnations. Plato, in particular, discussed the idea of reincarnation in his dialogues, suggesting that the soul's journey through multiple lives is a path toward greater knowledge and understanding.

In certain indigenous and tribal cultures, reincarnation plays a role in the continuity of the community. For example, some Native American tribes believe that the souls of ancestors can be reborn within the same family or tribe, ensuring the survival of the group's wisdom and traditions. Similarly, in some African and Australian Aboriginal cultures, it is believed that the spirits of the deceased return to the community through the birth of new children, maintaining a link between the past, present, and future generations.

Even within the Abrahamic religions, which traditionally emphasize a linear view of life and the afterlife, there have been historical instances where ideas resembling reincarnation were present. For instance, some early Christian sects, such as the Gnostics, believed in the pre-existence and reincarnation of the soul, though these views were later deemed heretical by the mainstream Church. In modern times, belief in reincarnation persists among certain Christian and Jewish mystics, as well as among individuals who identify with the broader concept of spiritual but not religious.

The Role of Reincarnation in Understanding Life and Death

Reincarnation offers a framework that profoundly shapes the way adherents understand life, death, and the human experience. In cultures and religions where reincarnation is a central belief, life is viewed as a temporary phase in a much longer, ongoing journey. Death, therefore, is not seen as an end but as a transition, a moment of passage from one state of existence to another.

This perspective can bring comfort to individuals facing the inevitability of death, providing a sense of continuity and the possibility of further opportunities for growth and fulfillment. It also offers explanations for the suffering and challenges individuals may face in life. Instead of seeing life's hardships as random or unjust, reincarnation provides a lens through which these experiences can be understood as the results of past actions or as necessary lessons for spiritual advancement.

Moreover, the belief in reincarnation can influence ethical behavior and moral decision-making. The awareness that one's actions in this life will affect future lives encourages a focus on virtue, compassion, and personal growth. It fosters a sense of responsibility, not only for oneself but for the collective welfare of all beings, as the cycle of birth and rebirth emphasizes the interconnectedness of all life.

IRREFUTABLE CASES

INTRODUCTION

Reincarnation, the belief that the soul or consciousness can be reborn into a new body after death, is a concept that has fascinated humanity for centuries. Among the most compelling evidence for reincarnation are the accounts of young children who claim to remember details of a previous life. These cases have been rigorously documented and studied by researchers, with Dr. Ian Stevenson being one of the most prominent figures in this field. Over decades, Stevenson collected and analyzed thousands of cases where children, often at a very young age, recounted vivid and specific memories of past lives. These accounts were often so detailed and verifiable that they challenged the conventional understanding of consciousness and the nature of human existence.

In this chapter, we will delve into several well-documented cases that Stevenson investigated, highlighting the evidence that supports the claims of these children. These cases, considered "irrefutable" by many in the field, provide a compelling argument for the possibility of reincarnation.

THE CASE OF SWARNLATA MISHRA

The case of Swarnlata Mishra is one of the most compelling and thoroughly documented instances of a child claiming to remember a past life. Born in 1948 in Pradesh, India, Swarnlata began exhibiting behaviors and recounting memories from a very young age that she claimed were from a previous life. What makes this case particularly intriguing is the specificity and accuracy of the details she provided, many of which were later verified, leading researchers to consider it as strong evidence for the possibility of reincarnation.

Swarnlata's Early Memories

Swarnlata was born into a relatively ordinary family, but from the age of three, she began to make statements that puzzled her parents. She claimed to have lived in a town called Katni, approximately 100 miles away from her current home. According to Swarnlata, in her previous life, she was a woman named Biya Pathak who had lived in a large house and had died at the age of 40. These claims were startling for a child of such a young age, especially considering that her family had no connection to Katni and no reason to discuss it.

As Swarnlata grew older, she provided increasingly detailed descriptions of her former life. She described the layout of the house she had lived in, including specific features such as the location of certain rooms, the furniture, and even the changes that had been made to the house after her death. Swarnlata also recalled the names of family members from her previous life, their relationships, and personal characteristics, all of which were unknown to her current family.

Verification of Swarnlata's Claims

In the 1950s, Dr. Ian Stevenson, a psychiatrist at the University of Virginia and a pioneering researcher in the field of reincarnation, learned of Swarnlata's case. Recognizing its potential significance, Stevenson decided to investigate her claims thoroughly. His investigation involved multiple visits to Swarnlata's home, extensive interviews with her family, and a detailed examination of the family she claimed to have belonged to in her previous life—the Pathak family of Katni.

One of the most striking aspects of Swarnlata's case was her ability to recognize members of the Pathak family when she met them for the first time. During a visit arranged by Stevenson, Swarnlata was introduced to several members of the Pathak family, who had traveled to her home. She immediately recognized each of them and addressed them using the correct names and terms of endearment that Biya Pathak would have used. For example, she identified her "husband," "son," and other relatives without any hesitation, and her emotional reactions were consistent with the relationships she described.

Swarnlata's recognition of these individuals was not limited to simple identification. She also recounted specific incidents and details about their lives that were later confirmed to be accurate. For instance, she described an incident where she had hidden money in a particular spot in the house, a fact that was unknown even to some current members of the Pathak family until they checked and found it exactly where she said it would be.

The Underground Vault

One of the most compelling pieces of evidence in Swarnlata's case involved her knowledge of an underground vault that had been built in the Pathak family's home. This vault was hidden and not known to many people, including some members of the Pathak family who were alive at the time of Swarnlata's birth. During her visit to Katni, Swarnlata accurately described the vault's location and purpose, much to the astonishment of the Pathak family. Her detailed description of the vault and its contents added significant weight to the argument that her memories were not fabricated or influenced by external sources.

Behavioral Evidence

In addition to the detailed memories she recounted, Swarnlata exhibited behaviors and mannerisms that were unusual for a child of her age and background but consistent with the personality and lifestyle of Biya Pathak. She demonstrated an unusual level of maturity and familiarity with customs and practices that were typical of an adult woman in her previous life, rather than a young child. For example, she showed a preference for certain foods and clothing styles that were characteristic of Biya Pathak. She also displayed a sense of authority and confidence when interacting with members of the Pathak family, behaving in a manner that was more befitting of an elder matriarch than a young girl.

These behavioral traits further supported the idea that Swarnlata's memories were genuine and not the result of fantasy or external influence. Her parents confirmed that she had not been exposed to the customs or practices she described before making these statements, making it unlikely that she had learned them through ordinary means.

Dr. Stevenson's Analysis

Dr. Stevenson's approach to investigating Swarnlata's case was methodical and rigorous. He conducted multiple interviews with Swarnlata, her current family, and the Pathak family, cross-referencing the details provided by Swarnlata with verifiable facts. Stevenson was particularly careful to rule out any possibility of fraud, suggestion, or coaching. He noted that the information Swarnlata provided was too specific and too accurate to be dismissed as mere coincidence or the result of overhearing adult conversations.

Stevenson's investigation also included an analysis of the psychological and social context of the case. He considered whether Swarnlata's claims could have been influenced by cultural factors or by a desire for attention. However, he found no evidence to suggest that Swarnlata had been encouraged or coached by her family. In fact, her parents were initially skeptical of her claims and only became convinced after witnessing the accuracy of her statements during the visits to Katni.

The consistency of Swarnlata's memories over time, combined with the lack of any apparent motive for deception, led Stevenson to conclude that her case provided strong evidence for reincarnation. He documented his findings in several publications, noting that Swarnlata's case was one of the most convincing examples he had encountered during his decades of research.

The Significance of the Swarnlata Mishra Case

The case of Swarnlata Mishra is significant for several reasons. First, it provides a compelling example of a child who not only claimed to remember a past life but also provided verifiable details that were unknown to her current family. The accuracy of her memories, particularly those involving specific incidents and hidden features of the Pathak family's home, makes it difficult to explain her knowledge through ordinary means.

Second, the case was thoroughly investigated by Dr. Ian Stevenson, whose reputation for rigorous research adds credibility to the findings. Stevenson's careful documentation of the case, including interviews with all involved parties and verification of the facts, provides a strong foundation for considering Swarnlata's memories as genuine.

Finally, the case challenges the conventional understanding of consciousness and memory. If Swarnlata's memories are indeed those of Biya Pathak, then this suggests that consciousness can survive physical death and be reborn in a new body, retaining memories from a previous life. This idea has profound implications for our understanding of the nature of the self and the continuity of consciousness.

In conclusion, the case of Swarnlata Mishra stands out as one of the most well-documented and convincing cases of reincarnation. The specificity of her memories, the accuracy of the details she provided, and the thorough investigation conducted by Dr. Stevenson make it a compelling piece of evidence in the study of life after death. While the case does not provide definitive proof of reincarnation, it offers strong support for the idea that consciousness may continue beyond a single lifetime, challenging us to reconsider our assumptions about life, death, and the nature of the human soul.

THE CASE OF JAMES LEININGER: A DETAILED EXAMINATION

The case of James Leininger is one of the most compelling and well-documented examples of a child remembering a past life, particularly in a modern, Western context where such claims are often met with skepticism. Born in 1998 in Louisiana, James began to display an intense interest in airplanes and military aviation at a very young age. This interest quickly escalated into a series of vivid nightmares and detailed statements about a previous life as a World War II fighter pilot. The accuracy and specificity of James's recollections, which were later verified through historical records and interviews with surviving veterans and relatives, make this case particularly significant in the study of reincarnation.

James's Early Memories and Nightmares

James Leininger's case first gained attention when he began having frequent nightmares around the age of two. These nightmares were unusually vivid and terrifying, involving scenes of being trapped in a burning airplane that was crashing. James would often wake up screaming about a plane crash, and his descriptions were unnervingly specific for a child of his age. He repeatedly mentioned details such as being shot down by the Japanese, his plane crashing into the water, and the inability to escape the burning wreckage.

James's parents, Bruce and Andrea Leininger, initially thought these nightmares were simply a phase, perhaps influenced by his fascination with airplanes. However, the nightmares persisted and were accompanied by detailed statements that seemed far beyond the realm of a toddler's imagination. James began to speak about a man named "Jack Larson" and an aircraft carrier called "Natoma." He also mentioned flying a specific type of aircraft—a Corsair—and claimed that he had been shot down over Iwo Jima during World War II.

Verification of James's Claims
At first, James's parents were skeptical of his claims. They assumed that his knowledge of these terms and names might have come from television or books, although they couldn't recall exposing him to any such material. However, as the details became more specific and consistent, they decided to investigate further.

Bruce Leininger, who initially dismissed his son's statements as childish fantasies, began to research the information James was providing. He discovered that "Natoma Bay" was indeed an aircraft carrier that had been involved in the Battle of Iwo Jima during World War II. Moreover, there was a record of a pilot named James M. Huston Jr., who had been killed in action during that battle. Huston had been flying a Corsair, just as young James had described, and his plane was shot down by Japanese fire, crashing into the Pacific Ocean.

The depth of James's knowledge about World War II aircraft and specific battles was extraordinary for a child of his age. He not only identified the type of plane Huston flew but also provided details about its unique characteristics, such as the difficulty Corsair pilots had with the aircraft's tendency to veer off to one side during takeoff. These details were later confirmed by military records and interviews with surviving veterans, including Jack Larson, whom James had mentioned by name. Larson had indeed served on the same aircraft carrier as James Huston Jr., and he was still alive when the Leiningers reached out to him.

Specific Details and Behavioral Evidence

James Leininger's case is not only compelling because of the specific factual details he provided but also because of the consistency with which he remembered these details over time. Unlike typical childhood fantasies that might change or fade, James's recollections remained consistent as he grew older. He continued to talk about his "previous life" as a fighter pilot, often providing new information that could be verified through historical records.

For instance, James described his plane being hit in the engine by Japanese fire, which caused it to crash. This matched the official military records of how James Huston Jr. had died. He also spoke of a particular friend and fellow pilot, Jack Larson, and correctly identified details about Larson's life and service that would have been impossible for a young child to know.

In addition to these specific memories, James exhibited behaviors that were unusual for a child of his age but consistent with someone who had a deep, innate knowledge of military aviation. He showed an exceptional interest in model airplanes, particularly those from the World War II era, and demonstrated an understanding of their mechanics that far exceeded what would be expected of a typical child. He also displayed a mature and somewhat somber demeanor when discussing his memories, as if recalling something deeply personal and significant.

One of the most striking pieces of evidence in this case was James's ability to accurately name various members of his previous "crew" and to describe events that were later verified by interviews with surviving veterans and military records. For example, when asked why he named his toy planes and drew pictures of aerial battles, James would respond with details about missions and fellow pilots, including names and locations that were later confirmed to be historically accurate.

Dr. Jim Tucker's Investigation

Dr. Jim Tucker, who succeeded Dr. Ian Stevenson in continuing research on children's past-life memories at the University of Virginia, became involved in James Leininger's case after hearing about it from the media. Dr. Tucker, known for his rigorous and methodical approach to investigating reincarnation cases, conducted a thorough examination of James's claims.

Dr. Tucker interviewed the Leininger family multiple times, carefully documenting James's statements and comparing them with historical records. He also reviewed the family's efforts to verify the information and spoke with surviving relatives and military personnel who could corroborate James's claims. Dr. Tucker concluded that the evidence strongly supported the possibility that James's memories were genuine and not the result of parental influence, prior exposure to this information, or fabrication.

In his analysis, Dr. Tucker noted that the likelihood of a child accurately recalling such specific and detailed information about a deceased World War II pilot, without having been exposed to this information through ordinary means, was extremely low. He also pointed out that James's parents had not encouraged or promoted his statements; on the contrary, they had initially been skeptical and had tried to discourage him from dwelling on these memories.

Dr. Tucker's findings were published in several academic papers and books, where he highlighted the James Leininger case as one of the most compelling modern examples of reincarnation. He argued that the consistency and specificity of James's memories, combined with the independent verification of his statements, made it one of the strongest cases for the survival of consciousness after death.

The Significance of the James Leininger Case

The case of James Leininger is significant for several reasons. First, it provides compelling evidence of reincarnation in a modern, Western context where such claims are less likely to be influenced by cultural or religious beliefs. The Leininger family had no prior interest in or exposure to reincarnation, making James's claims all the more remarkable.

Second, the level of detail and accuracy in James's memories far exceeds what could reasonably be attributed to coincidence or subconscious suggestion. His ability to recall specific names, locations, and events from a previous life, all of which were later verified through historical records and interviews, challenges conventional explanations and suggests that his memories may indeed be genuine.

Finally, the case highlights the importance of rigorous investigation and documentation in studying reincarnation. Dr. Jim Tucker's careful analysis of James's case, along with the thorough research conducted by James's parents, provides a strong foundation for considering this case as evidence for the possibility of reincarnation. The consistency of James's memories over time, combined with the independent verification of key details, makes it one of the most compelling examples of a child recalling a past life.

In conclusion, the case of James Leininger stands out as a powerful example of the potential for consciousness to survive death and be reborn in a new life. The detailed and verifiable nature of James's memories, along with the thorough investigation conducted by both his family and Dr. Tucker, make it a landmark case in the study of reincarnation.

THE CASE OF SHANTI DEVI: A DETAILED EXAMINATION

The case of Shanti Devi is one of the most extraordinary and well-documented instances of a child claiming to remember a past life. Born in 1926 in Delhi, India, Shanti began to speak about her previous life at the age of four, recounting detailed memories of her past existence in the town of Mathura, which was several hundred kilometers away from her home. Her case, investigated by multiple independent parties including Mahatma Gandhi, has stood the test of time as one of the most compelling pieces of evidence supporting the possibility of reincarnation.

SHANTI DEVI'S EARLY MEMORIES

From a young age, Shanti Devi began to express vivid memories of her previous life. She claimed that her name had been Lugdi Devi and that she had lived in Mathura with her husband, a man named Kedarnath Chaube. Shanti provided a wealth of specific details about her former life, including descriptions of her house, the layout of the neighborhood, and the circumstances of her death during childbirth. She spoke of her family, her daily routines, and even the food she used to eat—details that a young child in Delhi would have no way of knowing.

Shanti's parents, who had no connections to Mathura, were initially perplexed and skeptical of her claims. They dismissed her stories as the product of a vivid imagination or possibly overheard conversations. However, as Shanti continued to insist on the truth of her memories and provided increasingly specific details, her parents became concerned and eventually decided to investigate the matter further.

Verification of Shanti's Claims

As Shanti's parents began to look into the details she provided, they were astonished to discover that her statements corresponded closely with actual facts. They found that there was indeed a man named Kedarnath Chaube living in Mathura who had been married to a woman named Lugdi Devi. Lugdi had died during childbirth about a year before Shanti was born, just as Shanti had described.

Upon learning of Shanti's claims, Kedarnath was understandably curious and agreed to meet the child. In 1935, when Shanti was nine years old, a trip to Mathura was arranged. When Shanti arrived in Mathura, her behavior and knowledge of the town shocked everyone involved. She immediately recognized Kedarnath and several members of his family, addressing them by name and identifying their relationships to her from her previous life. This recognition was particularly impressive given that she had never met any of these people before, and her family had no previous contact with them.

Shanti's visit to Mathura included a tour of the house where Lugdi had lived. Shanti accurately described the layout of the house, pointing out specific features and identifying rooms that had been altered since Lugdi's death. She also recounted details of her previous life, such as personal possessions, events, and even intimate aspects of her relationship with Kedarnath, which were later confirmed by him. These were details that only Lugdi could have known, further reinforcing the credibility of Shanti's claims.

One of the most compelling aspects of Shanti's case was her ability to recognize and correctly describe places and objects in

Mathura that she had never seen before in her current life. For example, she accurately identified the location where she had hidden money in her previous life—a fact that had been known only to Lugdi and Kedarnath. Kedarnath himself was reportedly overwhelmed by the accuracy of Shanti's memories and acknowledged that she had described many details that were known only to him and his late wife.

The Investigation by Independent Parties

The case of Shanti Devi attracted considerable attention both in India and internationally. Given the significance of the claims, several independent parties conducted investigations to verify the authenticity of Shanti's memories. One of the most notable figures to take an interest in the case was Mahatma Gandhi, who was intrigued by the reports and decided to appoint a commission to study the case.

The commission, composed of fifteen prominent members including scholars, journalists, and politicians, undertook a thorough investigation. They interviewed Shanti, her family, Kedarnath, and other residents of Mathura. They also examined the locations and objects identified by Shanti and cross-referenced her statements with historical records.

The commission's findings were striking. They concluded that Shanti Devi's statements were highly accurate and could not be explained by normal means such as fabrication, suggestion, or prior knowledge. The report highlighted that Shanti had provided numerous details about her past life that were verified as true and that these details were so specific that it was unlikely she could have learned them through conventional means. The commission's report lent significant credibility to Shanti's claims and was widely publicized, further solidifying her case as one of the most convincing in the study of reincarnation.

Dr. Ian Stevenson's Analysis

Years later, Dr. Ian Stevenson, a psychiatrist at the University of Virginia and a leading researcher in the field of reincarnation, reviewed the case of Shanti Devi as part of his broader study of children who remember past lives. Stevenson was known for his meticulous approach to investigating such cases, and he recognized the Shanti Devi case as one of the most compelling examples of its kind.

In his analysis, Stevenson noted several key aspects of Shanti's case that made it particularly significant. First, the sheer volume of specific, verifiable details provided by Shanti, many of which were unknown to anyone outside the immediate family, strongly supported the authenticity of her memories. Second, the independent investigation by Gandhi's commission provided a level of scrutiny and credibility that few other cases of reincarnation had received.

Stevenson also pointed out that the cultural context in which the case occurred added another layer of complexity. While belief in reincarnation is common in India, the rigor with which Shanti's case was investigated helped to mitigate potential biases that might arise from cultural expectations. The consistency and accuracy of her memories, coupled with the corroboration from multiple independent sources, led Stevenson to conclude that Shanti Devi's case was one of the strongest pieces of evidence for reincarnation that he had encountered.

The Significance of the Shanti Devi Case

The case of Shanti Devi is significant for several reasons. First, it provides a well-documented example of a child who not only claimed to remember a past life but also provided a wealth of specific, verifiable details that were later confirmed through independent investigations. The accuracy of her memories, particularly those involving personal and intimate aspects of her previous life, make it difficult to dismiss her claims as mere coincidence or the result of external suggestion.

Second, the case was investigated by several independent parties, including a commission appointed by Mahatma Gandhi. The thoroughness of these investigations, along with the public nature of the findings, added a level of credibility and rigor to the case that is rare in the study of reincarnation. The commission's report, which concluded that Shanti's memories could not be explained by normal means, remains a crucial piece of evidence in support of her claims.

Finally, the Shanti Devi case challenges the conventional understanding of consciousness and memory. If her memories are indeed those of Lugdi Devi, then this suggests that consciousness can survive physical death and be reborn in a new body, retaining detailed memories from a previous life. This idea has profound implications for our understanding of the nature of the self and the continuity of consciousness.

In conclusion, the case of Shanti Devi stands as one of the most compelling and well-documented cases of reincarnation in the history of paranormal research. The detailed and accurate nature of her memories, the thorough investigation by multiple independent parties, and the cultural context in which the case occurred make it a landmark example of the possibility of reincarnation. While it may not provide definitive proof, it offers strong evidence that challenges our assumptions about life, death, and the nature of human consciousness, inviting further exploration into the mysteries of existence.

THE CASE OF GOPAL GUPTA: A DETAILED EXAMINATION

The case of Gopal Gupta is another fascinating example that adds to the growing body of evidence suggesting the possibility of reincarnation. Studied by Dr. Ian Stevenson, Gopal's case stands out due to the specific and verifiable details he provided about his past life as a boy named Suresh Verma, who had been murdered in a nearby village. The accuracy of Gopal's recollections, particularly concerning the circumstances of Suresh's death, makes this case particularly compelling and difficult to attribute to mere coincidence or imagination.

Gopal Gupta's Early Memories
Gopal Gupta was born in the early 1950s in India. From around the age of three, Gopal began to speak about his past life with startling clarity. He claimed that his previous name was Suresh Verma and that he had lived in a village not far from his current home. Gopal spoke in detail about his previous family, including the names of his parents, siblings, and other relatives. He also described the house where he had lived and provided specific details about the village and its surroundings.

What made Gopal's case particularly striking was his vivid recollection of the manner of his death. He claimed that in his previous life, he had been murdered. Gopal described the attack in detail, including the way he was ambushed and the injuries that led to his death. His descriptions were so precise that they included the exact location of the wounds and the type of weapon used. For a young child to speak with such specificity about such a traumatic event was both unusual and concerning for his parents.

Gopal's parents, who had no connections to the village he described and had no knowledge of the events he spoke about, were initially skeptical. However, as Gopal continued to insist on the accuracy of his memories and provided more details, his parents decided to investigate further. Their growing concern and curiosity led them to make the journey to the village Gopal claimed to have lived in as Suresh Verma.

The Visit to the Village and Verification of Claims

When Gopal and his parents arrived in the village that he claimed to have lived in during his previous life, the young boy's behavior was extraordinary. Despite never having visited the village before, Gopal immediately recognized the house he had described and confidently led his parents to it. Upon arriving, he accurately identified various members of Suresh Verma's family by name, even though he had never met them in his current life.

The family members were understandably astonished by Gopal's knowledge. He not only recognized them but also recounted specific details about his life as Suresh that only someone with intimate knowledge of the family would know. For instance, Gopal accurately described personal belongings, the layout of the house, and events that had occurred during Suresh's lifetime. These details were confirmed by Suresh's family, who were shocked by the accuracy of Gopal's statements.

One of the most compelling aspects of the case was Gopal's detailed knowledge of Suresh's murder. Gopal described how Suresh had been ambushed and attacked, and his account closely matched the medical records and police reports of the crime. He spoke of the location of the wounds and the type of weapon used, details that were consistent with the official investigation. The precision of Gopal's memories made it clear that he was recounting events with a level of accuracy that would be impossible for a young child to fabricate.

Dr. Ian Stevenson's Investigation
Dr. Ian Stevenson, a renowned psychiatrist and researcher in the field of reincarnation, took a keen interest in Gopal Gupta's case. Stevenson was known for his rigorous approach to investigating claims of past life memories, and he applied the same meticulous standards to Gopal's case. Stevenson's investigation involved multiple interviews with Gopal, his family, and Suresh Verma's family, as well as a thorough review of the medical and police records related to Suresh's death.

Stevenson was particularly impressed by the specificity of Gopal's recollections and the fact that so many of them could be independently verified. He found that many of the details Gopal provided were not known to his family and could not have been learned through ordinary means. For example, Gopal's descriptions of the murder scene and the events leading up to Suresh's death were corroborated by the records from the time of the crime. These details included not just the nature of the attack but also the exact sequence of events, the location where the murder took place, and the individuals involved.

Stevenson's investigation also involved examining possible alternative explanations for Gopal's memories. He considered the possibility of fraud, suggestion, or the influence of overheard conversations, but found no evidence to support these theories. Gopal's family had no prior knowledge of Suresh Verma or his family, and there was no indication that Gopal had been coached or influenced in any way. The consistency of Gopal's memories over time, combined with the verification of key details, led Stevenson to conclude that Gopal's case was a strong example of reincarnation.

The Significance of the Gopal Gupta Case

The case of Gopal Gupta is significant for several reasons. First, it provides compelling evidence of reincarnation in a cultural context where such beliefs are prevalent but where the rigor of investigation makes it difficult to dismiss the claims as merely culturally influenced. The accuracy of Gopal's memories, particularly those involving the details of Suresh Verma's murder, is difficult to explain through conventional means. The fact that Gopal could provide such specific information about people, places, and events he had never encountered in his current life challenges our understanding of memory and consciousness.

Second, Gopal's case was meticulously investigated by Dr. Ian Stevenson, whose work in the field of reincarnation is widely respected for its thoroughness and attention to detail. Stevenson's careful documentation and verification of Gopal's statements, combined with his consideration of alternative explanations, add a level of credibility to the case that is essential in the study of past life memories.

Finally, the Gopal Gupta case adds to the growing body of evidence suggesting that reincarnation may be a real phenomenon. The consistency of Gopal's memories, the specificity of the details he provided, and the independent verification of these details make it one of the most compelling cases in reincarnation research. It also highlights the possibility that consciousness can survive physical death and be reborn in a new body, retaining memories from a previous life.

Conclusion
The case of Gopal Gupta, along with those of Swarnlata Mishra, James Leininger, and Shanti Devi, represents some of the most well-documented and compelling instances of children remembering past lives. Dr. Ian Stevenson's meticulous research into these cases has provided a robust body of evidence that challenges the conventional understanding of consciousness and the finality of death.

These cases, with their detailed and verifiable information, suggest that reincarnation may indeed be a real phenomenon. The ability of these children to identify and accurately describe people, places, and events from previous lives that they could not have known through ordinary means provides strong support for the survival of consciousness after death. While these cases do not provide definitive proof of reincarnation, they offer compelling evidence that cannot be easily dismissed. They invite us to reconsider our understanding of life, death, and the nature of consciousness, and to remain open to the possibility that the soul or consciousness may continue to exist beyond a single lifetime. As research in this field continues, these irrefutable cases remain a cornerstone of the argument for reincarnation and the ongoing journey of the human soul.

Other studies done on the subject

1. Dr. Ian Stevenson's Research on Children's Past Life Memories
Study Overview: Dr. Ian Stevenson, a psychiatrist at the University of Virginia, is perhaps the most well-known researcher in the field

of reincarnation. Over four decades, Stevenson meticulously documented over 2,500 cases of children who claimed to remember past lives. His research primarily focused on cases where the children's statements about their previous lives were specific, detailed, and verifiable. He also examined physical evidence, such as birthmarks and congenital abnormalities that corresponded to injuries or other marks on the body of the deceased person the child claimed to have been.

Significance: Stevenson's work is considered groundbreaking for its rigor and the sheer volume of cases studied. His findings challenged the mainstream scientific view that consciousness is solely a product of the brain. The most compelling cases in his research involved children who provided specific details about past lives that could be verified through historical records or by locating the families of the deceased individuals they claimed to have been. These cases often included knowledge that the child could not have reasonably acquired through normal means. Stevenson's work has inspired further research into the phenomenon of reincarnation and remains a cornerstone in the field.

Key Publication:
Stevenson, I. (1974). Twenty Cases Suggestive of Reincarnation. University Press of Virginia.

2. Dr. Jim Tucker's Continuation of Stevenson's Work
Study Overview: Dr. Jim Tucker, also at the University of Virginia, has continued and expanded upon Ian Stevenson's research. Focusing on American cases, Tucker has explored children's past-life memories with the same rigorous methods Stevenson used. One of Tucker's notable cases involved a young boy named James Leininger, who provided detailed memories of being a World War

II fighter pilot. These memories included specific details about the plane he flew, his death, and the names of his fellow pilots, which were later confirmed to be accurate.

Significance: Tucker's work is significant because it brought the study of reincarnation into the modern era, particularly focusing on Western cases that are less likely to be influenced by cultural expectations of reincarnation. His research continues to provide compelling evidence that challenges the traditional understanding of consciousness, suggesting that past-life memories might be a real phenomenon deserving of serious scientific consideration.

Key Publication:

Tucker, J. B. (2005). Life Before Life: A Scientific Investigation of Children's Memories of Previous Lives. St. Martin's Press.

3. Dr. Erlendur Haraldsson's Study on Reincarnation in Sri Lanka

Study Overview: Dr. Erlendur Haraldsson, a psychologist from Iceland, conducted extensive research on reincarnation cases in Sri Lanka. He focused on children who claimed to remember past lives and, like Stevenson, worked to verify the details of these memories. Haraldsson's research included interviews with the children, their families, and the families of the deceased individuals the children claimed to have been.

Significance: Haraldsson's study is significant for its focus on a non-Western context where belief in reincarnation is culturally accepted. His findings provided additional support for the idea that children's memories of past lives are not simply the result of cultural influence or suggestion. The cases Haraldsson documented often included specific, verifiable details that were unknown to the children's families, further supporting the argument that these memories could be genuine recollections of past lives.

Key Publication:
Haraldsson, E. (1991). Children Who Speak of a Previous Life: A Psychological Investigation. University of Virginia Press.

4. Dr. Satwant Pasricha's Research on Reincarnation in India
Study Overview: Dr. Satwant Pasricha, an Indian psychologist, has conducted extensive research on reincarnation cases in India, often in collaboration with Ian Stevenson. Her work has focused on documenting cases where children report memories of past lives, particularly those that can be verified through detailed interviews and historical records. Pasricha's research is among the most comprehensive in terms of the number of cases studied and the depth of investigation.

Significance: Pasricha's research is significant for its systematic approach to studying reincarnation in a cultural context where the belief is widespread. By focusing on Indian cases, Pasricha has been able to explore the phenomenon in a society where reincarnation is an integral part of the belief system, while also employing rigorous scientific methods to ensure that cultural expectations do not unduly influence the results. Her findings have reinforced the view that some children's past-life memories are too specific and verifiable to be easily dismissed as fantasy or coincidence.

NEAR DEATH EXPERIENCE

Near-Death Experiences (NDEs) are among the most fascinating and perplexing phenomena reported by individuals who have come close to death or experienced a temporary cessation of vital functions. These experiences, often described in vivid detail, include sensations of leaving the body, moving through a tunnel toward a light, encountering deceased loved ones or spiritual beings, and gaining profound insights into the nature of life and death. NDEs challenge our conventional understanding of consciousness and suggest that the mind may continue to function even when the body is clinically dead.

In this chapter, we will delve into the phenomenon of Near-Death Experiences, exploring their common features, the profound effects they have on individuals, and the potential implications they hold for our understanding of consciousness and the possibility of life after death. We will examine a range of case studies, scientific research, and philosophical reflections that attempt to explain NDEs, offering a comprehensive overview of this extraordinary phenomenon.

One of the key aspects of NDEs is their consistency across different cultures, ages, and circumstances. Despite the wide variety of backgrounds and beliefs among those who report NDEs, the core elements of the experiences are remarkably similar. This consistency raises important questions about the nature of consciousness and whether it might transcend the physical body. Are NDEs merely the result of brain chemistry during the dying process, or do they provide a glimpse into a realm beyond our current understanding?

We will also consider the impact of NDEs on those who experience them. Many individuals report profound changes in their outlook on life, a decrease in fear of death, and an increased sense of spirituality or connection to the universe. These transformative effects suggest that NDEs are not simply hallucinations or the result of a dying brain, but rather significant events that can alter the course of a person's life.

Throughout this chapter, we will explore the various scientific theories proposed to explain NDEs, including neurological, psychological, and spiritual perspectives. We will also address the criticisms and counterarguments posed by skeptics, considering how these experiences fit into the broader framework of our understanding of consciousness and its potential survival after death.

By the end of this chapter, we aim to provide a balanced and in-depth exploration of Near-Death Experiences, offering insights into what they might reveal about the nature of consciousness and the possibility of an afterlife. Whether you approach this topic with curiosity, skepticism, or hope, the phenomenon of NDEs challenges us all to reconsider our assumptions about life, death, and what might lie beyond.

Common Factors in near death experience

Pim van Lommel, a renowned Dutch cardiologist, has extensively studied NDEs and provided valuable insights into their common elements. His research suggests that these experiences may offer a glimpse into the nature of consciousness and the possibility of an afterlife.

The Phenomenon of NDEs

Pim van Lommel's interest in NDEs began when he encountered patients who reported vivid experiences during cardiac arrest. Intrigued by their accounts, he conducted a large-scale study published in the medical journal "The Lancet" in 2001. Van Lommel's research revealed that NDEs are not merely hallucinations or the result of a dying brain but are consistent experiences reported by individuals across different cultures and backgrounds. His findings challenge conventional scientific views on consciousness, suggesting that it may exist independently of brain function.

COMMON ELEMENTS OF NDES

Van Lommel identified several common elements that characterize NDEs, regardless of the individual's cultural or religious background. These elements provide a framework for understanding the nature of these experiences and their potential implications for our understanding of life and death.

- Out-of-Body Experience (OBE)

One of the most frequently reported elements of an NDE is the sensation of leaving one's physical body. Individuals often describe floating above their bodies, observing medical personnel working to revive them. This out-of-body experience is typically accompanied by a sense of detachment and calmness. Van Lommel's research suggests that OBEs challenge the notion that consciousness is confined to the brain, indicating the possibility of consciousness existing independently of the physical body.

- Moving Through a Tunnel

Another common element of NDEs is the sensation of moving through a tunnel or passageway. This tunnel is often described as dark, with a bright light at the end. The experience of traveling through the tunnel is typically accompanied by feelings of peace and tranquility. Van Lommel notes that this element is consistent across different cultures, suggesting a universal aspect of the NDE experience.

- Encountering a Light

Many individuals who have experienced an NDE report encountering a bright, loving light at the end of the tunnel. This light is often described as being intensely beautiful and imbued with a sense of unconditional love and acceptance. Van Lommel's research indicates that this encounter with the light is a pivotal moment in the NDE, often leading to profound feelings of peace and joy.

- Life Review

A significant and transformative element of NDEs is the life review. During this experience, individuals report seeing their entire lives flash before them in a panoramic, three-dimensional review. This life review is not merely a recollection of events but involves re-experiencing emotions and the impact of one's actions on others. Van Lommel emphasizes that the life review often leads to a deeper understanding of the importance of love, compassion, and interconnectedness.

- Encountering Deceased Loved Ones

Many NDE experiencers report encounters with deceased loved ones or spiritual beings. These encounters are often described as joyful reunions, with the presence of these beings offering comfort and guidance. Van Lommel's research suggests that these encounters may indicate the continuity of consciousness beyond physical death, challenging traditional notions of the afterlife.

- A Sense of Returning to the Body

NDEs often conclude with a sense of being drawn back to the physical body. This return is sometimes accompanied by a reluctance to leave the peaceful, loving environment of the NDE.

However, individuals often report a sense of purpose or mission upon returning to life, feeling that they have been given a second chance to fulfill their life's purpose.

Implications of Van Lommel's Research
Pim van Lommel's research on NDEs has significant implications for our understanding of consciousness and the nature of existence. His findings challenge the traditional scientific view that consciousness is a product of brain activity, suggesting instead that consciousness may be a fundamental aspect of the universe, existing independently of the physical body.

Van Lommel's work also raises important questions about the nature of the afterlife. The common elements of NDEs, such as the life review and encounters with deceased loved ones, suggest that consciousness may continue after physical death. This challenges conventional religious notions of heaven and hell, proposing instead a more nuanced understanding of the afterlife as a realm of learning, growth, and interconnectedness.

Sources https://pimvanlommel.nl/

THE STORIES

THE CASE OF PAM REYNOLDS

Pam Reynolds' near-death experience (NDE) is one of the most compelling and well-documented cases in the study of consciousness and life after death. Her case is particularly significant because it occurred under highly controlled medical conditions, during which she was effectively in a state of clinical death. Despite this, Reynolds reported a vivid and detailed experience that included observations and perceptions that were later verified by the medical team involved in her surgery. The accuracy of her recollections, coupled with the fact that they occurred at a time when her brain was not functioning, challenges conventional explanations of NDEs and provides intriguing evidence for the possibility of consciousness existing independently of the physical brain.

Background and Medical Procedure

Pam Reynolds was a 35-year-old singer-songwriter from Atlanta, Georgia, when she was diagnosed with a life-threatening brain aneurysm in 1991. The aneurysm was located in her basilar artery, a critical blood vessel at the base of the brain, making the surgery to remove it extremely risky. The procedure chosen to address her condition was a "standstill" operation, also known as hypothermic cardiac arrest, which involved lowering her body temperature, stopping her heart, and draining the blood from her brain. This method would effectively induce a state of clinical death, allowing the surgeons to work on the aneurysm without the risk of blood flow causing it to rupture.

The operation was conducted at the Barrow Neurological Institute in Phoenix, Arizona, by Dr. Robert Spetzler, a renowned neurosurgeon. During the procedure, Reynolds' body temperature was reduced to 60 degrees Fahrenheit (about 15.5 degrees Celsius), her heart was stopped, and her brain activity was monitored to ensure that it had ceased. The medical team used electroencephalography (EEG) to confirm that there was no electrical activity in her brain, indicating that she was in a state of deep anesthesia with no possibility of conscious awareness. Additionally, auditory evoked potentials (AEPs) were used to ensure that her brainstem—responsible for basic functions like hearing—was inactive.

The Near-Death Experience

Despite being in this state of clinical death, Reynolds reported a vivid and coherent experience that began with a sense of floating out of her body and observing the surgical procedure from above. She described looking down on her own body as it lay on the operating table and observing the medical team as they prepared for the surgery. What makes her account particularly remarkable is her detailed descriptions of specific events and objects in the operating room—details that were later corroborated by the medical staff.

One of the most striking aspects of her experience was her description of the surgical instruments used during the procedure. Reynolds specifically mentioned a device that resembled an electric toothbrush, which she later identified as the bone saw used to open her skull. This device, known as a Midas Rex bone saw, was used to cut through her skull, and its unique sound was something she reported hearing even though her ears were blocked with molded earplugs that emitted a steady stream of loud clicks to monitor her brain activity. Her ability to describe the instrument, as well as the sound it made, is puzzling because, at the time, she had no brain activity that would allow her to hear or process sound.

Additionally, Reynolds accurately recalled conversations that took place in the operating room. She reported hearing a female voice say, "We have a problem. Her arteries are too small." This statement was confirmed by members of the surgical team, who had indeed discussed the difficulty they encountered due to the small size of her arteries, which complicated the insertion of the cannula used for bypass. The fact that Reynolds could recall this specific conversation, which occurred while she was clinically dead, is difficult to explain through conventional medical understanding.

Reynolds also described a sensation of moving through a tunnel toward a bright light, a common element in many NDE reports. She recounted feelings of peace and serenity and described encountering deceased relatives, including her grandmother, who communicated with her telepathically. These elements of her experience are consistent with many other NDE accounts, but what sets her case apart is the verifiable nature of the observations she made while her brain was not functioning.

Verification and Analysis

After the surgery, when Reynolds recounted her experience to the medical team, they were astounded by the accuracy of her descriptions. The surgical team confirmed that the details she provided about the instruments used, the conversations she overheard, and the sequence of events were accurate. Dr. Spetzler, who had performed the surgery, later stated that there was no physiological explanation for how Reynolds could have perceived these details, given that she was in a state of deep anesthesia and had no measurable brain activity.

The case of Pam Reynolds has been extensively analyzed by researchers and scholars interested in NDEs and the nature of consciousness. One of the key aspects of this case that makes it so compelling is the timing of Reynolds' experience. According to the medical records, her NDE occurred during the period when her brain was effectively shut down, with no electrical activity detectable by the EEG. This detail is crucial because it challenges the hypothesis that NDEs are merely the result of residual brain activity or hallucinations occurring in a dying brain.

Skeptics have proposed alternative explanations, such as the possibility that Reynolds' NDE occurred during the induction or recovery phases of anesthesia, when some level of brain activity might still have been present. However, this explanation fails to account for the specific details she described that occurred while her brain was clinically inactive. Furthermore, the content of her experience—such as the accurate descriptions of surgical instruments and conversations—does not align with typical anesthesia awareness, a phenomenon where patients regain consciousness during surgery but usually experience it as confusion or panic, rather than coherent and verifiable observations.

Another skeptical argument is that Reynolds might have somehow heard the conversations and the sounds of the surgery through the bone conduction of sound, despite the earplugs and the brain monitors. However, this hypothesis is weakened by the fact that she accurately identified the Midas Rex bone saw, an instrument she had never seen or heard of before the surgery, and described its sound in a manner consistent with its operation.

The Implications of Pam Reynolds' NDE

Pam Reynolds' near-death experience has significant implications for our understanding of consciousness and its potential independence from the brain. Her case challenges the materialistic view that consciousness is solely a product of brain activity and suggests the possibility that consciousness can persist and perceive even when the brain is non-functional.

If consciousness can indeed exist independently of the brain, as Reynolds' case suggests, it raises profound questions about the nature of the self and what happens after death. The veridical aspects of her NDE—those elements that were observed and later verified—provide strong evidence that consciousness might continue in some form after the physical body ceases to function.

Reynolds' experience also contributes to the broader body of NDE research, which consistently reports similar themes of out-of-body experiences, encounters with deceased loved ones, and a sense of moving toward a light. The consistency of these reports across different cultures and time periods adds weight to the argument that NDEs are not merely hallucinations or brain-induced fantasies, but potentially glimpses into a reality that transcends our current understanding of life and death.

Conclusion

The case of Pam Reynolds remains one of the most compelling pieces of evidence in the study of near-death experiences and the nature of consciousness. The detailed and verifiable nature of her observations during a period when her brain was inactive challenges conventional explanations and suggests that consciousness may not be entirely dependent on the physical brain.

As researchers continue to explore the phenomenon of NDEs, cases like that of Pam Reynolds provide valuable insights into the possibility of life after death and the true nature of human consciousness. While this case does not provide definitive proof, it offers compelling evidence that invites further exploration into the mysteries of consciousness and its potential to exist beyond the boundaries of the physical body.

THE CASE OF MARIA'S SHOE

The case of Maria's Shoe is one of the most intriguing and frequently cited examples of veridical perception in near-death experiences (NDEs). It involves a woman named Maria who, following a heart attack, reported leaving her body and observing her surroundings from a vantage point that should have been impossible given her physical location and condition. What makes this case particularly compelling is the discovery of a physical object—a shoe—that Maria claimed to have seen during her out-of-body experience (OBE). The precise details of this object, its location, and the fact that it was found exactly as Maria described, lend significant credibility to her account and raise important questions about the nature of consciousness and its relationship to the physical body.

Background and Maria's Near-Death Experience

In the late 1970s, Maria, a migrant worker, was admitted to Harborview Medical Center in Seattle after suffering a severe heart attack. During her time in the hospital, Maria experienced a profound NDE. She later recounted that during this experience, she felt herself leave her body and rise above the hospital room, observing the medical team as they worked to revive her. From this elevated perspective, Maria claimed to be able to see not only the activities in the room but also objects and events occurring outside the immediate environment of her physical body.

One of the most striking aspects of Maria's NDE was her description of a shoe she observed on a ledge outside the hospital building. According to Maria, this shoe was located on a third-floor ledge and was positioned in such a way that it was not easily visible from the ground or from the hospital rooms. She described the shoe in detail, noting that it was a dark blue tennis shoe with a worn toe and a shoelace tucked under the heel.

After Maria was resuscitated and stabilized, she shared her experience with Kimberly Clark, a social worker at the hospital. Maria insisted that she had seen this shoe while she was "out of her body" and asked Clark to check if it was actually there. Skeptical but curious, Clark agreed to investigate.

Verification of the Shoe's Existence

Kimberly Clark's search for the shoe began with a tour of the area Maria had described. Clark initially had difficulty locating the shoe because it was not in a place that would be easily visible from the ground or from any of the nearby windows. However, after some effort, she eventually found the shoe on the ledge exactly as Maria had described it. The shoe was indeed a dark blue tennis shoe, just as Maria had reported. The details Maria provided—such as the worn appearance of the toe and the position of the shoelace—matched the shoe's actual condition perfectly.

What made this discovery so significant was the fact that the shoe was located in a position where it would have been nearly impossible for Maria to have seen it from her hospital room or any other normal vantage point. The ledge where the shoe was found was on the outside of the building, and the shoe was positioned in such a way that it was not visible from the ground level. The only way Maria could have seen the shoe, given its location, was if she had indeed been observing the scene from an elevated, out-of-body perspective as she claimed.

Clark was astounded by the accuracy of Maria's description and by the fact that the shoe was found in such an unlikely location. The verification of this detail added a level of credibility to Maria's entire NDE account that would have been difficult to achieve through other means. Clark documented the incident and shared her findings with other researchers, making the case of Maria's Shoe one of the most well-known examples of veridical perception in the study of NDEs.

The Significance of Veridical Perception

The concept of veridical perception—where a person accurately perceives events or objects in the physical world while in an altered state of consciousness—is a critical area of interest in NDE research. Cases like Maria's Shoe challenge the conventional understanding of consciousness as being confined to the brain and reliant on the body's sensory organs for perception. If Maria's account is taken at face value, it suggests that her consciousness was able to function and observe her surroundings independently of her physical body, even while she was clinically dead or unconscious.

This case is significant because it provides tangible, verifiable evidence that supports the idea that consciousness can exist outside of the physical body. Unlike many NDE accounts that involve subjective experiences such as encounters with spiritual beings or feelings of peace, Maria's experience includes a specific, objectively verifiable detail—the location and condition of the shoe—that can be confirmed by others. This level of verification is rare in NDE research and makes Maria's case particularly valuable to those studying the nature of consciousness.

The implications of veridical perception are profound. If consciousness can indeed perceive the physical world without the use of the body's sensory organs, it challenges the materialistic view that consciousness is solely a byproduct of brain activity. Instead, it suggests that consciousness may have a non-local aspect, capable of existing and perceiving independently of the brain and body. This idea aligns with some of the more radical theories of consciousness, such as non-local consciousness or dualism, which propose that the mind or soul is distinct from the physical brain and can exist beyond it.

Skeptical Explanations and Counterarguments

As with all extraordinary claims, the case of Maria's Shoe has faced scrutiny and skepticism. Some skeptics have proposed alternative explanations for Maria's experience, suggesting that she might have seen the shoe before her heart attack, either consciously or unconsciously, and then incorporated it into her NDE. However, this explanation is weakened by the fact that the shoe was located in a place that was difficult to see from any normal perspective, including the hospital room or common areas. Furthermore, Maria's description of the shoe's specific details, such as the worn toe and tucked-in shoelace, suggests a level of observation that would have been unlikely even if she had seen the shoe beforehand.

Another skeptical argument is that the shoe's discovery might have been a coincidence or the result of suggestion. For instance, critics might argue that Maria's account influenced Clark's search, leading her to find a shoe that matched the description through confirmation bias. However, this argument fails to account for the fact that Maria's description was made before any search took place and that the shoe was found exactly where Maria said it would be, on a ledge outside the hospital, where it was unlikely to be seen by anyone inside the building.

Moreover, the fact that Kimberly Clark was initially skeptical and had difficulty finding the shoe suggests that she was not predisposed to confirming Maria's account. The shoe was located after a deliberate search, and its discovery matched the specific details provided by Maria, lending credibility to her claim that she observed the shoe while out of her body.

Implications and Conclusion

The case of Maria's Shoe remains one of the most intriguing examples of veridical perception in NDE research. The fact that Maria accurately described an object in a location that would have been impossible for her to see under normal circumstances adds significant weight to her account and challenges the conventional understanding of consciousness. If Maria's experience is accepted as genuine, it suggests that consciousness can exist and perceive independently of the physical body, raising profound questions about the nature of life, death, and what happens to consciousness after the body ceases to function.

This case, along with other similar accounts, invites us to reconsider our assumptions about the relationship between the mind and the body. While not definitive proof of an afterlife, the case of Maria's Shoe provides compelling evidence that consciousness may have capabilities that go beyond our current scientific understanding. As researchers continue to explore the mysteries of NDEs and veridical perception, cases like this one offer valuable insights into the potential for consciousness to transcend the physical limits of the body, opening new avenues for understanding the true nature of human experience and existence.

THE CASE OF DR. EBEN ALEXANDER

The case of Dr. Eben Alexander is one of the most intriguing and controversial examples of a near-death experience (NDE), largely because of his background as a neurosurgeon and the severe medical condition under which his experience occurred. In 2008, Dr. Alexander, who had previously been a skeptic of NDEs and dismissed them as the result of brain chemistry, underwent a profound transformation after he himself experienced an NDE while in a coma induced by severe bacterial meningitis. His account, which he detailed in his bestselling book Proof of Heaven, describes a journey to a realm of consciousness that he claims could not have been the product of his severely compromised brain.

Background and Medical Condition

Dr. Eben Alexander's journey into what he describes as a "heavenly realm" began when he contracted a rare and aggressive form of bacterial meningitis, Escherichia coli meningitis, which is particularly devastating in adults. The infection severely damaged his neocortex, the part of the brain responsible for higher functions such as sensory perception, motor commands, spatial reasoning, conscious thought, and language. Within hours of being admitted to the hospital, Alexander slipped into a deep coma as the infection ravaged his brain, leaving him with little hope of survival. His condition was so severe that his chances of recovery were estimated to be less than 10%, and his brain activity, as measured by various clinical tests, was significantly diminished, with almost no signs of higher cortical function.

During the seven days that Dr. Alexander remained in a coma, his family was preparing for the worst. His physicians, who knew the grim prognosis associated with such extensive brain damage, were skeptical that he would ever regain consciousness, let alone recover fully. Yet, against all odds, Dr. Alexander did eventually wake up. Not only did he survive, but he also made a full recovery—an outcome that, in itself, is considered medically remarkable. However, what he recounted after regaining consciousness is what has made his case a focal point in the discussion about the nature of consciousness and the afterlife.

Dr. Alexander's Near-Death Experience

While in the coma, Dr. Alexander reported having an experience that he described as more real and vivid than anything he had ever encountered in his waking life. He recounted his NDE as a journey through a series of realms, beginning with a dark, murky underworld that he referred to as the "Realm of the Earthworm's Eye View." In this state, he felt as though he was submerged in a primordial, muddy environment, lacking any sense of time or self-awareness.

From this dark and foreboding place, Dr. Alexander was then "rescued" by a brilliant light accompanied by a musical melody, which he followed upward. He found himself in a stunning, idyllic landscape filled with vibrant colors, blooming flowers, and angelic beings. He described being in the presence of a divine, all-loving being that he identified as God or an aspect of the divine. He also encountered a beautiful, young woman who served as his guide during the experience, who he later believed to be a deceased sibling he had never met in life. The woman communicated with him telepathically, conveying messages of love, reassurance, and the interconnectedness of all things.

Dr. Alexander emphasized that the experiences he had during this time were not dreamlike or hallucinatory, but were instead hyper-real, with a clarity and depth that surpassed ordinary consciousness. He described how he felt an overwhelming sense of peace, love, and acceptance—emotions that he had never experienced so profoundly before. He also reported receiving insights into the nature of the universe and the purpose of life, which he struggled to fully articulate upon his return to his physical body.

Perhaps most strikingly, Dr. Alexander argued that the vividness and complexity of his NDE could not have been produced by his brain, given the extent of his cortical damage. The neocortex, which is responsible for generating and processing conscious experience, was severely compromised, rendering it highly unlikely—if not impossible—that it could produce the kind of detailed and structured experiences he reported.

The Medical and Scientific Context

What makes Dr. Eben Alexander's case particularly compelling is his extensive medical background and understanding of the brain. Prior to his NDE, Alexander had spent years as a practicing neurosurgeon, and he was well-versed in the physiological functions of the brain. He had previously subscribed to the materialistic view that consciousness is solely a product of brain activity, and that NDEs are likely the result of chemical processes in a dying brain—hallucinations or fantasies created by the release of endorphins or other neurochemicals in times of extreme stress.

However, his own experience profoundly challenged this view. Given his understanding of the brain's function, Alexander found it difficult to reconcile his NDE with the severely impaired state of his cortex during his coma. According to conventional medical science, with his neocortex in such a damaged state, his brain should not have been capable of producing any conscious experiences, let alone the rich, detailed, and coherent journey he described.

Critics of Alexander's account have suggested alternative explanations, such as the possibility that his NDE occurred during the recovery phase, as his brain was regaining function, or that it was a form of "rebooting" of the brain as it started to heal. However, Alexander contends that his experiences could not have occurred during those times, as his medical records show no significant brain activity that could account for the level of consciousness he described.

Additionally, some neuroscientists argue that even in cases of severe brain injury, the brain might still produce fragmentary or residual activity that could result in vivid experiences, particularly during transitions between states of consciousness. However, the complexity and coherence of Alexander's NDE, especially given the extent of his brain damage, remain difficult to explain under this framework.

The Implications of Dr. Alexander's Experience

Dr. Alexander's NDE has significant implications for the ongoing debate about the nature of consciousness and the possibility of an afterlife. If his account is taken at face value, it suggests that consciousness might not be entirely dependent on the physical brain and could continue to exist even when the brain is severely impaired or non-functional. This idea aligns with theories of non-local consciousness, which propose that consciousness is not confined to the brain but is a fundamental aspect of the universe, potentially surviving beyond physical death.

Alexander's experience also challenges the materialistic view that NDEs are simply the result of neurochemical processes in a dying brain. Instead, his account points to the possibility that NDEs might represent genuine experiences of a different realm of consciousness, one that is not bound by the limitations of the physical brain. His background as a neurosurgeon adds credibility to his claims, as he approaches the phenomenon with a deep understanding of the brain's workings, making his insights particularly valuable.

Dr. Alexander's case has sparked considerable interest and debate within both the scientific community and the general public. It has been featured in numerous interviews, documentaries, and academic discussions, and has inspired many people to reconsider their views on life, death, and the nature of consciousness. His book, Proof of Heaven, became a bestseller and has been translated into multiple languages, further spreading his message and encouraging others to explore the mysteries of consciousness and the afterlife.

Criticisms and Counterarguments

Despite the widespread attention and support for Dr. Alexander's account, his experience has also faced criticism from some in the scientific community. Skeptics argue that his NDE could still be explained by the residual or re-emerging activity in his brain, even if his neocortex was severely damaged. They suggest that the brain, even in a compromised state, could produce vivid, dream-like experiences as it attempts to recover or during moments of partial awakening.

Others have pointed out that NDEs often reflect the cultural and personal beliefs of the experiencer, raising questions about whether these experiences are truly universal or if they are shaped by individual expectations and prior knowledge. In Dr. Alexander's case, some critics have suggested that his experience might have been influenced by his own subconscious mind, drawing on his existing knowledge and beliefs about life and death.

However, Dr. Alexander has consistently countered these criticisms by emphasizing the unprecedented vividness, coherence, and structure of his NDE, which he believes cannot be explained by any known neurological mechanisms given the state of his brain at the time. He also notes that his experience led to a profound personal transformation, which is a common feature of many NDEs and is often cited as evidence of their authenticity.

Conclusion

The case of Dr. Eben Alexander stands as one of the most compelling and controversial examples of a near-death experience, particularly because of his medical background and the severe condition of his brain during the event. His account challenges conventional scientific explanations for NDEs and suggests the possibility that consciousness might exist independently of the brain, potentially surviving physical death.

Whether one views Dr. Alexander's experience as proof of an afterlife or as a phenomenon that still requires further investigation, it undeniably contributes to the ongoing debate about the nature of consciousness and the limits of human understanding. His story invites us to explore the profound mysteries of existence and to remain open to the possibility that consciousness might extend beyond the boundaries of the physical world, offering a glimpse into realms yet to be fully understood.

Near-Death Experiences (NDEs) are remarkable not only for their vivid and often transformative nature but also for the intriguing evidence they sometimes provide for the survival of consciousness beyond physical death. Below are several examples of NDEs that include particularly compelling evidence, such as consciousness during anesthesia, the return of sight in blind individuals, and instances of deathbed lucidity.

Consciousness During Anesthesia: The Case of Al Sullivan

Al Sullivan, a middle-aged man, experienced an NDE while undergoing heart surgery under general anesthesia. Sullivan's heart stopped during the operation, leading to a temporary cessation of blood flow to his brain. Under normal circumstances, general anesthesia should prevent any awareness, as the brain is not supposed to be capable of processing experiences during deep anesthesia, especially when blood flow is disrupted.

However, Sullivan reported a vivid NDE during this time. He described floating above his body and observing the surgical team as they worked on him. He provided specific details about the procedure, including the types of instruments used and conversations between the doctors. Sullivan even recounted seeing his surgeon flapping his arms like a chicken—a behavior the surgeon later confirmed as something he did to avoid contaminating his hands after they had been scrubbed.

This case is significant because it occurred during a period when Sullivan's brain should not have been capable of conscious awareness, especially under the influence of anesthesia and during cardiac arrest. The accuracy of his observations and the fact that they were later corroborated by the medical team add weight to the argument that his consciousness persisted independently of his physical brain.

Return of Sight in Blind Individuals: The Case of Vicki Umipeg

Vicki Umipeg (later Vicki Noratuk) was born blind due to severe eye damage from premature birth. She had never experienced vision and did not have the ability to perceive light or shadows. However, at the age of 22, Vicki was involved in a severe car accident that led to an NDE. During her experience, she reported having clear, vivid vision for the first time in her life.

Vicki described floating above her body and seeing herself lying on a stretcher in the hospital emergency room. She also observed the efforts of the medical staff to revive her, describing their actions, clothing, and equipment in detail. After floating through the hospital, she experienced moving through a tunnel toward a light and encountering deceased relatives who appeared to her in their physical forms.

Vicki's account is particularly compelling because, as someone who had been blind from birth, she had no prior visual reference or memories to draw upon. Her ability to describe visual scenes accurately, including the people and objects in the room, challenges conventional explanations and suggests that her consciousness accessed a form of perception beyond the limitations of her physical senses.

Deathbed Lucidity: The Case of Lydia Helene

Lydia Helene, a woman in her late 80s, had been suffering from severe dementia for several years, rendering her almost completely uncommunicative and mentally unaware. Her cognitive decline was so advanced that she was unable to recognize her own family members or engage in coherent conversation. However, just days before her death, Lydia experienced a sudden and profound return of mental clarity, a phenomenon known as deathbed lucidity.

During this period of lucidity, Lydia astonished her family and caregivers by suddenly recognizing and addressing them by name, engaging in meaningful conversations, and reminiscing about past events with complete accuracy. She expressed joy at seeing her family and conveyed a sense of peace and acceptance about her impending death. This period of lucidity lasted for several hours before she peacefully passed away.

Deathbed lucidity is particularly significant because it occurs in individuals whose brains have been severely compromised by conditions such as dementia, Alzheimer's disease, or brain injuries. The sudden and temporary return of mental clarity in these individuals, often just before death, challenges our understanding of the brain's role in consciousness and suggests that the mind may be capable of functioning independently of the physical state of the brain.

THE COMMON FACTORS IN NDE'S

Pim van Lommel is a Dutch cardiologist best known for his pioneering research on near-death experiences (NDEs) and consciousness. His work has significantly contributed to the understanding of consciousness as a non-local phenomenon, which means that consciousness may exist independently of the brain and body. Although van Lommel's research primarily focuses on NDEs, his findings have important implications for the study of reincarnation, as they suggest that consciousness can survive bodily death, potentially supporting the concept of rebirth.

In his landmark study published in The Lancet in 2001, van Lommel examined NDEs in patients who had been clinically dead for a short period but were successfully resuscitated. His research showed that a significant number of these patients reported vivid experiences that seemed to occur during the time when their brains were not functioning, challenging the conventional materialistic view of consciousness as solely a product of brain activity. Van Lommel's findings open the door to discussions about the survival of consciousness after death and, by extension, the possibility of reincarnation.

Researchers like Dr. Raymond Moody, Dr. Bruce Greyson, Dr. Pim van Lommel, and others have dedicated their careers to studying NDEs, bringing this once-taboo subject into the scientific spotlight. Their work has documented thousands of cases across different cultures, religions, and backgrounds, revealing common patterns and experiences that cannot be easily dismissed as mere hallucinations or the byproducts of a dying brain.

Dr. Raymond Moody: Often credited with bringing NDEs to public attention, Moody's book "Life After Life" highlighted the similarities in NDEs across diverse individuals, sparking widespread interest and further research.

Dr. Bruce Greyson: A psychiatrist who developed the "Greyson Scale" to measure the depth and characteristics of NDEs, Greyson's work has provided a framework for systematically studying these experiences.

Despite their extensive research and the consistency of their findings, these pioneers of NDE research have not been able to provide a definitive explanation for the phenomena they have studied. The evidence they have gathered points to the limitations of current scientific theories and the need for a new understanding of consciousness.

7.3 THE LIMITS OF CONVENTIONAL THEORIES

Modern science offers several theories to explain NDEs, but none are sufficient to account for all the documented phenomena. These theories include:

- Oxygen Deprivation (Hypoxia): Some suggest that NDEs are the result of oxygen deprivation in the brain. However, this theory does not explain why individuals report heightened awareness, vivid perceptions, and clear thinking during NDEs—states that should be impossible under conditions of severe hypoxia.

- Anoxia-Induced Hallucinations: Another theory posits that NDEs are hallucinations caused by the brain's dying process. Yet, this fails to account for the consistency of NDE reports across different cultures and individuals, and the fact that many NDEs include verifiable observations that are later confirmed by others.

- Endorphin Release: Some propose that NDEs are triggered by the brain's release of endorphins during traumatic events, leading to a euphoric state. However, this does not explain the experiences of individuals who accurately report events that occurred around them while they were unconscious or clinically dead.

These theories, while offering partial explanations, fall short in addressing the full scope of NDE phenomena, particularly the most compelling cases where individuals perceive events from a vantage point outside their bodies or report verifiable details that they could not have known through normal sensory perception.

PERCEPTION WITHOUT A BRAIN

One of the most puzzling aspects of NDEs is how individuals with little or no measurable brain activity can perceive their surroundings with greater clarity than ever before. For instance, there are well-documented cases where individuals under general anesthesia—who then suffer cardiac arrest—report waking up after being clinically dead, able to describe in detail what occurred during the period when they were supposedly unconscious and unresponsive.

Out-of-Body Experiences (OBEs) During NDEs: Many NDEs include OBEs, where individuals report seeing their own bodies from above, often describing the actions of medical personnel or the environment around them with astonishing accuracy. These accounts challenge the materialist view that consciousness is entirely dependent on brain function.

Veridical Perception: In some cases, individuals who were clinically dead or in a deep coma have described events occurring in another room or far away from their physical bodies—events that were later corroborated by independent witnesses. This phenomenon raises serious questions about the nature of consciousness and its potential independence from the physical brain.

The Continuation of Awareness: Perhaps most intriguingly, many who experience NDEs report that their awareness continued after all signs of brain activity had ceased. This continuation of consciousness, despite the brain being in a state where such experiences should be impossible, suggests that consciousness may not be entirely dependent on the brain's physical processes.

THE IMPLICATIONS: A CHALLENGE TO MODERN SCIENCE

The findings from NDE research point to something extraordinary: consciousness may not be as tightly bound to the physical body as we have traditionally believed. If consciousness can exist independently of the brain, as NDEs suggest, then our understanding of life, death, and the very nature of reality needs to be reconsidered.

A Call for a New Paradigm: The current materialist model of science, which views consciousness as a byproduct of brain activity, struggles to explain the phenomena associated with NDEs. Accepting the evidence for NDEs requires a paradigm shift—one that acknowledges the possibility that consciousness might persist beyond physical death.

Resistance from the Scientific Community: Despite the compelling nature of NDE research, many in the scientific community remain skeptical, largely because accepting these findings would necessitate rewriting much of what is currently understood about the brain and consciousness. Medical textbooks, neuroscience theories, and even our understanding of human identity would need to be re-evaluated.

The Need for Further Research: The resistance to these ideas highlights the need for more rigorous and open-minded research. While the evidence for NDEs is strong, particularly in cases involving veridical perception, more studies are needed to explore the mechanisms behind these experiences and their implications for our understanding of consciousness.

7.6 Conclusion: The Unanswered Questions of NDEs

The study of Near-Death Experiences raises profound questions that challenge our deepest assumptions about life, death, and consciousness. While no single theory can fully explain what happens at the moment of death, the consistency and strangeness of NDE reports suggest that something extraordinary is occurring—something that our current scientific models are not equipped to explain.

These experiences, documented in countless studies, point to the possibility that consciousness can survive without a body. Yet, modern science has difficulty accepting this, as doing so would require a fundamental shift in how we understand the brain, consciousness, and the nature of reality itself.

- Van Lommel, P. (2001). "Near-death experience in survivors of cardiac arrest: A prospective study in the Netherlands." The Lancet, 358(9298), 2039-2045.
- Van Lommel, P. (2010). Consciousness Beyond Life: The Science of the Near-Death Experience.
- Tucker, J. B. (2005). Life Before Life: A Scientific Investigation of Children's Memories of Previous Lives.
- Greyson, B. (2003). "Near-death experiences in a psychiatric outpatient clinic population." Psychiatric Services, 54(12), 1649-1653.
- Moody, R. A. (1975). Life After Life: The Investigation of a Phenomenon—Survival of Bodily Death.

OUT-OF-BODY EXPERIENCES (OBES) AND REMOTE VIEWING

REMOTE VIEWING

Remote viewing, a phenomenon that has garnered significant attention and controversy, poses a formidable challenge to the conventional scientific community. This practice, which involves perceiving and describing a target, such as a location or object, without the use of one's physical senses, has been the subject of extensive research and debate. In this chapter, we will delve into the definition and history of remote viewing, the CIA's interest in and studies on the subject, the Star Gate program, and the key findings and implications that have emerged from this research.

DEFINITION AND HISTORY OF REMOTE VIEWING

Remote viewing is a technique that allows an individual to gather information about a target, which can be a location, object, or person, without the use of their physical senses. This is achieved through a process of focused attention, relaxation, and concentration, which enables the individual to access and describe the target in detail. The practice of remote viewing has its roots in the 1970s, when physicists Russell Targ and Harold Puthoff conducted experiments at Stanford Research Institute (SRI) to investigate the phenomenon of psychic espionage.

THE CIA'S INTEREST IN AND STUDIES ON REMOTE VIEWING

In the 1970s, the Central Intelligence Agency (CIA) became interested in remote viewing as a potential tool for gathering intelligence. The agency saw the potential for remote viewing to provide a means of accessing information about enemy targets without the need for physical surveillance. The CIA's interest in remote viewing led to the establishment of the Star Gate program, a secret research project that aimed to investigate the military applications of remote viewing.

THE STAR GATE PROGRAM

The Star Gate program was a CIA-funded research project that ran from 1978 to 1995. The program was established to investigate the military applications of remote viewing and to develop a team of remote viewers who could provide intelligence on enemy targets. The program was led by physicist Edwin May, who had previously worked with Targ and Puthoff at SRI. The Star Gate program involved a team of remote viewers who were trained to use their abilities to gather information about targets, which were often located in enemy territory.

KEY FINDINGS AND IMPLICATIONS

The research conducted under the Star Gate program yielded some remarkable results, which challenged the conventional scientific understanding of perception and consciousness. Some of the key findings include:

- Accuracy of Remote Viewing: Studies conducted under the Star Gate program demonstrated that remote viewing could be used to gather accurate information about targets, even when the viewer had no prior knowledge of the target.
- Non-Local Perception: The research suggested that remote viewing was a form of non-local perception, which allowed the viewer to access information about a target without the need for physical proximity.

- Consciousness and Perception: The findings of the Star Gate program challenged the conventional understanding of consciousness and perception, suggesting that the human mind was capable of accessing information about the world in ways that were not previously understood.

The implications of the Star Gate program's findings are significant, and they challenge the conventional scientific understanding of perception and consciousness. The research suggests that the human mind is capable of accessing information about the world in ways that are not previously understood, and that remote viewing may be a valuable tool for gathering intelligence and accessing information about the world.

OUT-OF-BODY EXPERIENCES

Out-of-Body Experiences (OBEs) represent one of the most intriguing and mysterious phenomena in the study of consciousness. Often described as moments when an individual perceives themselves as existing outside their physical body, OBEs challenge our fundamental understanding of the relationship between mind and body. Whether occurring spontaneously during life-threatening situations or being induced through various techniques, OBEs offer compelling evidence that consciousness may possess the ability to transcend the physical confines of the human body.

This chapter delves into the definition and characteristics of OBEs, explores the distinction between spontaneous and induced experiences, and examines instances of veridical perception during OBEs that suggest the independence of consciousness from the body. By investigating these aspects, we aim to uncover the potential implications of OBEs for our broader understanding of consciousness and reality.

Definition and Characteristics of OBEs

What Are Out-of-Body Experiences?

An Out-of-Body Experience (OBOE) is a phenomenon in which an individual perceives themselves as existing outside their physical body, often observing their own body and the surrounding environment from a vantage point outside of it. This experience can vary in intensity and duration, ranging from fleeting moments of disembodiment to prolonged periods of external observation.

- **Sensory Perception**: During an OBE, individuals typically report heightened sensory awareness. They may describe seeing their physical body from an external perspective, observing their immediate environment with clarity, and sometimes perceiving events or locations beyond their physical presence.
- **Altered Consciousness**: OBEs are often accompanied by a sense of altered consciousness, where the individual's awareness shifts from their physical self to an external point of view. This shift can involve a feeling of floating, flying, or moving through space without the constraints of gravity or physical limitations.
- **Emotional and Psychological Impact**: Many individuals who experience OBEs report profound emotional and psychological effects, such as a sense of peace, heightened awareness, or spiritual enlightenment. Conversely, some may experience fear or disorientation,

especially if the experience is unexpected or uncontrollable.

Common Features of OBEs

While OBEs can vary widely among individuals, several common features are frequently reported:

- **Autoscopic Perception**: A hallmark of OBEs is the ability to see one's own physical body from an external viewpoint, often with a sense of detachment.
- **Vivid Sensory Detail**: Observers often describe their surroundings with remarkable detail, sometimes noting elements that are not visible or accessible to them in their physical state.
- **Movement and Travel**: Many report the ability to move freely in the external space, often traveling to distant locations instantaneously or over extended periods.
- **Temporal Dissociation**: Time perception may be altered, with individuals experiencing a sense of timelessness or disconnection from the passage of time in their physical body.
- **Return to the Body**: The experience typically concludes with a return to the physical body, which may be abrupt or gradual, leaving the individual with lingering impressions of the OBE.

Spontaneous and Induced OBEs

OBEs can occur spontaneously or be intentionally induced through various practices. Understanding the different contexts in which OBEs arise can provide insight into their nature and potential mechanisms.

Spontaneous OBEs

Spontaneous OBEs occur without any deliberate attempt to induce them. They are often reported in situations of extreme stress, trauma, or near-death experiences (NDEs).

- **Near-Death Experiences**: Many OBEs are associated with NDEs, where individuals who have been close to death report experiencing a separation from their body, often accompanied by sensations of peace, light, and the presence of otherworldly beings. These experiences are sometimes interpreted as evidence of an afterlife or the soul's ability to exist independently of the body.
- **Traumatic Events**: In the wake of traumatic events, such as accidents or violent encounters, some individuals report experiencing OBEs as a coping mechanism, providing a sense of detachment and safety from the immediate physical danger.
- **Sleep and Dreams**: OBEs can also occur during altered states of consciousness associated with sleep, such as lucid dreaming or sleep paralysis. In these states, the boundary between wakefulness and dreaming becomes blurred, facilitating experiences of disembodiment.

Induced OBEs

Induced OBEs are deliberately sought through various techniques aimed at separating consciousness from the physical body. These methods are often rooted in spiritual, mystical, or psychological practices.

- **Meditation and Mindfulness**: Deep meditation practices can lead to altered states of consciousness where individuals feel a sense of separation from their physical form. Techniques focusing on breath control, visualization, and concentration are commonly used to induce OBEs.
- **Sensory Deprivation**: Practices such as flotation tanks or sensory deprivation chambers reduce external stimuli, allowing the mind to enter a relaxed state conducive to OBEs. The absence of sensory input can facilitate the detachment of consciousness from the body.
- **Binaural Beats and Brainwave Entrainment**: Audio techniques that use binaural beats to synchronize brainwave activity can help individuals achieve the relaxed, meditative states necessary for inducing OBEs. These auditory stimuli can guide the brain into frequencies associated with deep relaxation and altered consciousness.
- **Pharmacological Methods**: Certain substances, including psychedelics or dissociative agents, can alter consciousness and potentially induce experiences akin to OBEs. However, these methods carry significant risks and ethical considerations.
- **Hypnosis and Guided Imagery**: Hypnotherapy and guided visualization techniques can facilitate OBEs by leading individuals into altered states of consciousness where they can visualize or experience detachment from their physical bodies.

COMPARATIVE ANALYSIS: SPONTANEOUS VS. INDUCED OBES

While both spontaneous and induced OBEs share common features, they differ in their triggers, contexts, and potential outcomes.

- **Triggers and Contexts**: Spontaneous OBEs are often linked to extreme conditions or natural occurrences, whereas induced OBEs are the result of intentional practices aimed at achieving disembodiment.
- **Control and Predictability**: Induced OBEs may offer individuals more control over the experience, allowing for intentional exploration of consciousness. In contrast, spontaneous OBEs are unpredictable and may occur without warning, sometimes causing distress or confusion.
- **Purpose and Intent**: Induced OBEs are frequently pursued for personal growth, spiritual exploration, or psychological healing. Spontaneous OBEs, on the other hand, may serve as protective mechanisms or be interpreted as glimpses into other realms or dimensions.

Veridical Perception During OBEs (the same as in NDE)

One of the most compelling aspects of OBEs is the occurrence of veridical perception, where individuals report accurate information about their environment or distant locations that they could not have accessed through their physical senses. These instances provide potential evidence for the independence of consciousness from the physical body.

Defining Veridical Perception in OBEs

Veridical perception refers to the accurate perception of information that is otherwise inaccessible through normal sensory channels. In the context of OBEs, this might involve:

- **Perceiving Hidden Objects or Events**: Observers report seeing objects, locations, or events that are not present or visible to their physical body at the time of the experience.
- **Accurate Descriptions of Distant Locations**: Individuals may describe distant geographic locations with surprising accuracy, including specific details that they could not have known through conventional means.
- **Information Beyond Sensory Limits**: Perceptions of events occurring in different times or places, including details that are later verified as accurate, suggest that consciousness can access information beyond the physical realm.

Notable Cases of Veridical Perception in OBEs

Several documented cases highlight instances of veridical perception during OBEs:

- **Clinical Studies**: In controlled clinical settings, some individuals have reported accurate descriptions of hidden targets while in an OBE state. For example, during experimental sessions, participants describe specific details of objects or environments that are not visible to them physically but are later verified to be accurate.

- **Anecdotal Reports**: Numerous anecdotal accounts from individuals who have experienced OBEs include descriptions of specific events or locations that they were unaware of at the time, only to have these details confirmed later.
- **Historical and Cultural Accounts**: Throughout history, various cultural and spiritual traditions include accounts of OBEs where individuals perceive information about other places or times that are later corroborated.

12.4.3 SCIENTIFIC INVESTIGATIONS AND FINDINGS

Scientific investigations into veridical perception during OBEs have produced mixed results, but some studies suggest that these perceptions cannot be easily dismissed as mere hallucinations or cognitive biases.

- **Laboratory Experiments**: Controlled experiments have been conducted to test the validity of veridical perceptions during OBEs. In some cases, participants accurately describe hidden targets or provide information that is later confirmed to be correct, suggesting that their consciousness accessed information beyond their physical senses.
- **Meta-Analyses**: Meta-analyses of multiple studies have found that, while the majority of OBE reports do not include veridical perception, there is a statistically significant number of instances where the information provided by individuals during OBEs matches real-world targets with a higher frequency than chance would predict.

- **Criticisms and Alternative Explanations**: Critics argue that veridical perceptions can be explained by factors such as sensory leakage, information leakage, or statistical anomalies. They caution that the evidence for independence of consciousness remains inconclusive and that more rigorous research is needed to rule out alternative explanations.

Implications of Veridical Perception for Consciousness Studies

If veridical perception during OBEs is reliably demonstrated, it has profound implications for our understanding of consciousness and its relationship to the physical body.

- **Non-Local Consciousness**: Veridical perceptions suggest that consciousness may operate on a non-local level, meaning it is not confined to a specific physical location or tied directly to the brain's neural networks.
- **Mind-Body Dualism**: These findings lend support to dualistic theories of consciousness, which posit that the mind or soul exists independently of the body, capable of existing and functioning outside of the physical form.
- **Challenging Materialism**: The possibility that consciousness can access information beyond the physical senses challenges materialistic views that see consciousness as entirely emergent from brain activity. It suggests that there may be more to consciousness than currently understood physical processes.
- **Expanding Scientific Paradigms**: Veridical perceptions during OBEs encourage the scientific community to broaden its paradigms and consider new models that

incorporate the potential for non-physical aspects of consciousness.

Empirical Research and Evidence

The study of OBEs and veridical perception has garnered interest across multiple disciplines, leading to various research efforts aimed at understanding and validating these experiences.

Laboratory Studies on OBEs

Controlled laboratory studies have attempted to induce and measure OBEs to better understand their nature and underlying mechanisms.

- **OBOE Induction Techniques**: Researchers have employed techniques such as virtual reality, sensory deprivation, and brain stimulation to induce OBE-like experiences in participants. These studies aim to replicate the sensations and perceptions reported in spontaneous OBEs to investigate their causes.
- **Measurement and Verification**: Some experiments have attempted to test the veridical perception aspect of OBEs by presenting hidden targets or objects to participants during their experiences. The accuracy of participants' descriptions is then evaluated against the actual targets to assess the validity of their perceptions.
- **Findings**: While some studies report instances of accurate target descriptions beyond chance levels, the results are often inconsistent and subject to methodological criticisms. Replicability remains a significant challenge in this field of research.

Field Studies and Anecdotal Evidence

Beyond laboratory settings, field studies and anecdotal reports contribute to the body of evidence supporting OBEs and veridical perception.

- **Case Studies**: Detailed accounts of individuals experiencing OBEs in real-world settings provide qualitative data on the nature and content of these experiences. These case studies often highlight patterns and commonalities across different individuals and contexts.
- **Surveys and Questionnaires**: Large-scale surveys collecting self-reported experiences of OBEs help identify prevalence rates, common triggers, and associated characteristics. These studies can reveal correlations between OBEs and various psychological, physiological, and environmental factors.
- **Cross-Cultural Comparisons**: Comparing OBE reports across different cultures and traditions can shed light on universal aspects of the phenomenon and cultural variations in interpretation and meaning.

Implications for Understanding Consciousness and Reality

The study of OBEs and veridical perception has profound implications for our understanding of consciousness, reality, and the potential boundaries of human perception.

Rethinking the Nature of Consciousness

OBEs challenge the traditional view that consciousness is solely a product of the brain's physical processes. If consciousness can exist independently of the body and access information beyond sensory limitations, it suggests that consciousness may have properties that are not fully accounted for by current scientific models.

- **Expanded Consciousness Models**: The possibility of non-local consciousness encourages the development of more expansive models that incorporate both physical and non-physical aspects of the mind.
- **Integration with Neuroscience**: Understanding OBEs could lead to new insights into how consciousness interacts with the brain, potentially revealing unknown mechanisms or dimensions of mental processing.
- enlightenment, and connect with higher states of consciousness.

THE CIA'S INTEREST IN PARANORMAL PHENOMENA

During the height of the Cold War, the United States and the Soviet Union engaged in a relentless competition for technological, military, and intelligence superiority. In this climate of rivalry and suspicion, the Central Intelligence Agency (CIA) became increasingly interested in exploring unconventional methods of gaining an advantage, including the investigation of paranormal phenomena such as Out-of-Body Experiences (OBEs) and Remote Viewing. The possibility that these phenomena could be harnessed for espionage and intelligence purposes led to a series of experiments and studies funded by the CIA, aimed at understanding and potentially exploiting these abilities.

This chapter explores the motivations behind the CIA's interest in OBEs and Remote Viewing, details the key experiments and studies conducted by the agency, and examines the outcomes and implications of their investigations, including the involvement of notable figures like Ingo Swann.

Motivation Behind the CIA's Interest in OBEs and Remote Viewing

The Cold War Context

The CIA's interest in OBEs and Remote Viewing was largely motivated by the geopolitical tensions of the Cold War. As reports surfaced that the Soviet Union was investing in research related to psychic phenomena, including telepathy, psychokinesis, and ESP (extrasensory perception), the CIA grew concerned that these abilities could be used against the United States in espionage or military operations.

- **Intelligence Gathering**: The CIA saw the potential for Remote Viewing to be used as a tool for intelligence gathering, allowing operatives to access information about enemy installations, military plans, or secret locations without physically being present. If successful, this method could provide a significant strategic advantage.
- **Psychological Warfare**: There was also interest in the psychological implications of OBEs and Remote Viewing. If these phenomena could be weaponized, they could be used to manipulate or destabilize opponents by creating uncertainty or fear regarding the United States' capabilities.

- **Defense Against Soviet Research**: The CIA's interest was not solely offensive; there was also a defensive aspect. If the Soviets were indeed making advances in psychic phenomena, the CIA needed to understand these capabilities to develop countermeasures or protective strategies.

Exploration of Human Potential

Beyond the immediate military and intelligence motivations, the CIA's interest in OBEs and Remote Viewing was also part of a broader exploration of human potential. During the 1960s and 1970s, there was growing interest in the untapped abilities of the human mind, influenced by the countercultural movement, Eastern spiritual practices, and new scientific theories that challenged traditional materialistic views.

- **Mind Over Matter**: The CIA was intrigued by the possibility that the mind could influence physical reality in ways that defied conventional understanding. If OBEs and Remote Viewing were genuine, they could offer insights into the capabilities of human consciousness and its interaction with the physical world.
- **Expanding the Limits of Intelligence**: By exploring OBEs and Remote Viewing, the CIA hoped to expand the limits of intelligence gathering, moving beyond traditional methods like surveillance and espionage to more esoteric and potentially more powerful techniques.

Experiments and Studies Conducted by the CIA

The CIA funded and conducted a series of experiments and studies to investigate the potential of OBEs and Remote Viewing, often collaborating with leading researchers and psychics in the field. These efforts culminated in several key projects and programs.

Project Stargate

Project Stargate is perhaps the most well-known CIA initiative involving Remote Viewing and OBEs. This program, which began in the 1970s and continued through the early 1990s, was a classified research effort aimed at exploring the use of psychic phenomena for intelligence purposes.

- **Origins of Stargate**: Project Stargate evolved from earlier CIA projects such as SCANATE (Scanning by Coordinate) and GRILL FLAME, which were focused on developing methods for Remote Viewing. These initial projects demonstrated enough promise to warrant further investigation and expansion, leading to the establishment of Stargate as a broader program.
- **Goals and Objectives**: The primary goal of Project Stargate was to assess the feasibility of using Remote Viewing for gathering intelligence on military and strategic targets. The program also explored the potential of OBEs for similar purposes, though Remote Viewing was the main focus.
- **Scope and Scale**: At its height, Project Stargate involved numerous participants, including military personnel, civilian researchers, and psychics. The program

conducted hundreds of sessions, targeting a wide range of locations and events, from Soviet military installations to domestic criminal investigations.

The Role of Ingo Swann

One of the most significant figures in the CIA's investigation of Remote Viewing was Ingo Swann, a noted psychic and artist who played a central role in developing the protocols and techniques used in the Stargate program.

- **Swann's Contributions**: Ingo Swann was instrumental in shaping the methodology of Remote Viewing, particularly the concept of "coordinate Remote Viewing," where viewers attempt to describe a target location based solely on its geographic coordinates. Swann's work demonstrated a high degree of accuracy in several key experiments, which helped to validate the potential of Remote Viewing in the eyes of the CIA.
- **Notable Experiments**: One of Swann's most famous experiments involved Remote Viewing of the planet Jupiter before the Pioneer 10 spacecraft provided detailed images. Swann accurately described features such as Jupiter's ring system, which was later confirmed by the spacecraft's data. This experiment, though not directly related to intelligence gathering, showcased the potential of Remote Viewing to access information beyond conventional sensory means.
- **Collaboration with Hal Puthoff and Russell Targ**: Swann worked closely with physicists Hal Puthoff and Russell Targ at the Stanford Research Institute (SRI), where much of the Remote Viewing research funded by the CIA took

place. Together, they developed the protocols that would become the foundation of the Stargate program.

Remote Viewing Experiments

The CIA's Remote Viewing experiments were designed to test the accuracy and reliability of Remote Viewing as a method for gathering intelligence. These experiments involved a range of targets, from military bases to specific individuals, and were conducted under controlled conditions to minimize the possibility of sensory leakage or other forms of bias.

- **Coordinate Remote Viewing (CRV)**: One of the key techniques developed during these experiments was Coordinate Remote Viewing (CRV), where participants were given the geographic coordinates of a target and asked to describe the location and its features. The results were then compared to actual photographs or on-the-ground reports to assess accuracy.
- **Target Selection**: The targets for these experiments were often chosen randomly and were unknown to the viewers at the time of the session. This was intended to prevent any preconceived notions or prior knowledge from influencing the results. Targets ranged from secret Soviet facilities to more mundane locations, such as American landmarks.
- **Successes and Challenges**: While many of the Remote Viewing sessions produced results that were remarkably accurate, there were also many failures and inconsistencies. The success rate varied depending on the viewer, the target, and the conditions of the experiment. Despite these challenges, the CIA continued to fund and

support the research, believing that even a small success rate could be valuable in certain intelligence contexts.

Remote Viewing Experiments: Successes and Implications

The Remote Viewing experiments conducted by the CIA yielded a number of successes that, while not conclusive, suggest that the phenomenon may have some validity. These successes have important implications for our understanding of consciousness and the potential for human perception to transcend conventional limits.

Notable Successes in Remote Viewing

- **Soviet Military Installations**: In one series of Remote Viewing experiments, participants were able to describe secret Soviet military installations with surprising accuracy, providing details that were later confirmed by satellite imagery and other intelligence sources. These successes demonstrated the potential value of Remote Viewing for gathering intelligence on foreign adversaries.
- **Domestic Applications**: In addition to military targets, Remote Viewing was also used in domestic cases, such as locating missing persons or solving criminal cases. While the results were not always successful, there were instances where Remote Viewing provided leads or insights that proved useful to investigators.
- **Cross-Cultural Targets**: Remote Viewing experiments also explored the ability to perceive distant or culturally unfamiliar locations. In some cases, viewers were able to describe locations in other countries that they had never visited, with a degree of accuracy that suggested a

genuine perception beyond the normal sensory capabilities.

Implications for Consciousness Studies

The successes in Remote Viewing experiments raise important questions about the nature of consciousness and its potential to operate independently of the physical senses.

- **Non-Local Consciousness**: The ability to perceive distant locations or events suggests that consciousness may not be confined to the brain or the body. Instead, it may operate on a non-local level, capable of accessing information beyond traditional sensory boundaries.
- **Challenges to Materialism**: The results of the CIA's Remote Viewing experiments challenge the materialistic view of consciousness, which holds that all mental processes are rooted in physical brain activity. If Remote Viewing is genuine, it implies that consciousness can interact with the world in ways that are not fully understood by current scientific models.
- **Potential for Future Research**: While the Stargate program was terminated, the findings from the Remote Viewing experiments continue to inspire interest and research in the field of consciousness studies. These experiments suggest that there may be untapped potentials within the human mind that could be explored through further investigation.

Conclusion: The Legacy of the CIA's Investigation of OBEs and Remote Viewing

The CIA's investigation of Out-of-Body Experiences (OBEs) and Remote Viewing represents a unique chapter in the history of intelligence and consciousness research. Motivated by the Cold War context and the desire to explore unconventional methods of intelligence gathering, the CIA funded and conducted a series of experiments that yielded both successes and challenges.

While the Stargate program ultimately concluded that Remote Viewing was not reliable enough for operational use, the findings from these experiments continue to provoke interest and debate. The successes in Remote Viewing suggest that there may be more to human consciousness than is currently understood, challenging traditional scientific models and opening the door to new possibilities in the study of the mind.

As we move forward, the legacy of the CIA's investigation serves as a reminder of the importance of open-minded exploration and the need to balance curiosity with rigor and ethical considerations. The potential for consciousness to operate beyond the physical body remains a tantalizing mystery, one that may hold the key to unlocking new dimensions of human perception and understanding.

Sources

1. A Perceptual Channel for Information Transfer over Kilometer Distances: Historical Perspective and Recent Research" by Harold Puthoff and Russell Targ, Proceedings of the IEEE (1976)

2. "Out-of-Body Experiences: Neurological Mechanisms and Implications for Neurophilosophy" by Olaf Blanke and Shahar Arzy, Journal of Neuropsychology (2005)
3. "Out-of-Body Experiences: A Phenomenological Comparison of Spontaneous and Experimentally Induced Cases" by Carlos S. Alvarado, Journal of Near-Death Studies (2000)
4. "Stargate: The U.S. Government's Secret Attempt to Harness Psychic Power" by David Hambling, Wired (2017

Declassified Government Documents

1. "CIA-RDP96-00788R001900760001-9: An Overview of the Stargate Project"
2. "CIA-RDP96-00788R001700210016-5: Summary of Assessment of Remote Viewing Programs"

DEATHBED VISIONS AND SHARED DEATH EXPERIENCES

Introduction: Encounters at the Edge of Life

As individuals approach the end of life, there are numerous reports of extraordinary experiences that seem to provide comfort and insight into what might lie beyond death. Among these phenomena, deathbed visions and shared death experiences stand out as particularly compelling. Deathbed visions occur when individuals who are nearing death report seeing deceased loved ones, religious figures, or other comforting presences, often accompanied by feelings of peace and acceptance. Shared death experiences, on the other hand, are reported by those who are present at the moment of someone else's death and who experience similar phenomena, such as seeing a light or feeling a profound sense of euphoria.

These experiences suggest that there may be a transitional phase of consciousness as the soul prepares to leave the physical body, offering a glimpse into a potential afterlife or the continuity of consciousness beyond death. This chapter explores the characteristics of deathbed visions and shared death experiences, examines the evidence supporting these phenomena, and considers their implications for our understanding of consciousness and the dying process.

Deathbed Visions: Encounters with the Departed

Defining Deathbed Visions

Deathbed visions, also known as end-of-life experiences (ELEs), occur when individuals who are close to death report seeing or communicating with deceased loved ones, religious figures, or other comforting presences. These visions are typically described as vivid and real, providing comfort to the dying individual and often leading to a sense of peace and acceptance regarding their impending death.

- **Common Characteristics**:
    - **Appearance of Deceased Loved Ones**: Many individuals report seeing family members or friends who have passed away. These figures often appear healthy, radiant, and reassuring, offering messages of comfort and encouragement.
    - **Religious or Spiritual Figures**: Some individuals report seeing religious or spiritual figures, such as angels, saints, or even deities, who convey a sense of divine presence and support.
    - **Peaceful and Positive Emotions**: Deathbed visions are almost universally accompanied by feelings of peace, love, and acceptance. The fear of death often diminishes, replaced by a sense of calm and readiness to transition.
- **Timing and Context**: These visions typically occur in the final days or hours of life, often during periods of lucidity, even in patients who may have been previously unresponsive or in a state of delirium. The clarity and consistency of these experiences have intrigued researchers and caregivers alike.

Historical and Cultural Perspectives

Deathbed visions are not a new phenomenon; they have been documented throughout history and across cultures, often interpreted within the context of religious or spiritual beliefs.

- **Ancient and Religious Texts**: Historical accounts of deathbed visions can be found in ancient texts and religious scriptures, where they are often seen as evidence of an afterlife or the soul's journey after death. For example, in Christianity, deathbed visions are sometimes viewed as glimpses of heaven or encounters with guardian angels.
- **Cross-Cultural Accounts**: Different cultures interpret deathbed visions in various ways, but they are generally seen as positive and reassuring experiences. In Hinduism, for instance, such visions might be understood as part of the soul's transition to its next life, while in many Indigenous traditions, these visions are seen as visits from ancestors guiding the individual to the spirit world.

Evidence and Research

Research into deathbed visions has been conducted primarily through qualitative studies, including interviews with hospice workers, caregivers, and family members who have witnessed or heard about these experiences.

- **Hospice and Palliative Care Studies**: Many hospice workers report that a significant number of their patients experience deathbed visions. These professionals note that such experiences often lead to a more peaceful and

less traumatic death, both for the individual and for their loved ones.
- **Case Studies**: Numerous case studies document instances where dying individuals have described seeing deceased loved ones or religious figures. These reports are often consistent across different individuals and settings, lending credibility to the phenomenon.
- **Skeptical Perspectives**: While many find these experiences compelling, skeptics argue that deathbed visions could be the result of physiological processes in the dying brain, such as the release of endorphins or changes in oxygen levels. However, the subjective reality and consistency of these experiences suggest that there may be more to them than just physiological explanations.

Shared Death Experiences: Witnessing the Transition

Defining Shared Death Experiences

Shared death experiences (SDEs) occur when individuals who are present at the moment of someone else's death report experiencing phenomena similar to those described in near-death experiences (NDEs). These phenomena can include seeing a light, feeling a sense of euphoria, or even perceiving the soul leaving the body.

- **Common Characteristics**:
    - **Perception of Light**: Witnesses of shared death experiences often report seeing a bright light or glowing presence in the room at the moment of death.

- - **Feelings of Euphoria**: Those who experience SDEs frequently describe a sudden, overwhelming sense of peace, love, or euphoria, as if they are sharing in the transition of the dying person.
  - **Visual or Auditory Phenomena**: Some individuals report seeing the soul or spirit of the deceased leaving the body, often accompanied by ethereal sounds or music.
- **Involuntary Participation**: Unlike near-death experiences, which occur to individuals who are themselves close to death, shared death experiences happen to bystanders—often family members, friends, or caregivers—who are not in any immediate danger of dying themselves.

Historical and Anecdotal Accounts

Shared death experiences, while less commonly documented than deathbed visions, have been reported throughout history and across cultures.

- **Historical References**: Historical accounts of shared death experiences can be found in religious texts, folklore, and literature. These experiences are often interpreted as signs of a deep spiritual connection between the dying individual and the witness.
- **Anecdotal Reports**: Many contemporary accounts of shared death experiences come from loved ones who were present at the time of death. These witnesses often describe their experiences as profoundly spiritual and

life-changing, providing them with comfort and a sense of connection to the deceased.

Research and Implications

Research into shared death experiences is still in its early stages, but the phenomenon has attracted the attention of those studying consciousness, death, and the afterlife.

- **Dr. Raymond Moody's Research**: One of the most well-known researchers in this area, Dr. Raymond Moody, has written extensively about shared death experiences. In his book "Glimpses of Eternity," Moody documents numerous cases of SDEs and explores their implications for our understanding of death and consciousness.
- **Implications for Consciousness Studies**: Shared death experiences challenge the traditional view that consciousness is confined to the individual brain. If multiple people can experience similar phenomena at the moment of death, it suggests that consciousness may be more interconnected than previously thought, potentially extending beyond the individual.
- **Ethical and Clinical Considerations**: The study of shared death experiences also raises important questions for hospice and palliative care. Understanding these experiences could help caregivers provide better support to the dying and their families, acknowledging the spiritual and emotional dimensions of the dying process.

The Implications of Deathbed Visions and Shared Death Experiences

The phenomena of deathbed visions and shared death experiences offer profound insights into the nature of consciousness and the process of dying. While these experiences are not universally accepted by the scientific community, they provide compelling evidence that consciousness may persist beyond physical death, challenging materialistic views of the mind.

Support for the Continuity of Consciousness

Both deathbed visions and shared death experiences suggest that consciousness may continue in some form after the physical body ceases to function. These experiences are often described as vivid, real, and transformative, providing comfort to the dying and their loved ones. The consistency and positive nature of these reports lend credence to the idea that there is a transitional phase of consciousness as the soul prepares to leave the body.

- **Challenges to Materialism**: These phenomena challenge the materialistic view that consciousness is purely a product of brain activity. If consciousness can perceive and interact with the world in ways that transcend the physical body, it suggests that the mind may have a non-physical component that survives death.
- **Potential Evidence for an Afterlife**: For many, deathbed visions and shared death experiences provide a glimpse of what might lie beyond death, offering potential evidence for an afterlife or the continuation of the soul. These experiences often align with cultural and religious beliefs about the afterlife, reinforcing their significance for those who witness them.

A NEW VISION OF THE AFTERLIFE

Throughout this book, we've delved into various paranormal phenomena such as Out-of-Body Experiences (OBEs), Near-Death Experiences (NDEs), deathbed visions, and Remote Viewing. These experiences challenge our conventional understanding of consciousness and suggest that our existence may extend beyond the material world. When considered together, these phenomena point toward the possibility of an afterlife, although one that may differ significantly from traditional religious conceptions like Heaven or Hell.

In this chapter, we will draw from the evidence provided by these experiences to propose a new vision of the afterlife. By examining the common threads across NDEs, OBEs, and related phenomena, we can begin to outline what might happen after we die. This vision diverges from traditional religious narratives, proposing instead a more complex and continuous process of learning, growth, and self-reflection. Moreover, we will explore how future theories about consciousness and the afterlife might integrate these findings to offer a more complete understanding of what lies beyond death.

Glimpses of the Afterlife Through Near-Death Experiences

One of the most compelling pieces of evidence for an afterlife comes from Near-Death Experiences (NDEs). Individuals who have undergone NDEs often report profound encounters with light, deceased loved ones, and a sense of leaving their physical bodies behind. These experiences offer a glimpse into what the afterlife might entail.

A common feature in many NDEs is the **life review**, where individuals relive significant moments from their lives, often experiencing the emotions and perspectives of others involved. This suggests that the afterlife may involve a deep reflection on one's actions and their impact on others. Rather than being a moment of final judgment, this review seems to foster growth and understanding.

Another recurring element in NDEs is the encounter with **beings of light**. These entities, often described as spiritual guides or aspects of a higher consciousness, offer guidance and reassurance. Unlike the traditional image of a judgmental deity, these beings appear to focus on healing and learning. Those who experience NDEs frequently describe an overwhelming sense of **peace, love, and acceptance**, which contrasts sharply with the fear of punishment or judgment commonly associated with religious depictions of the afterlife.

The Evidence from Out-of-Body Experiences and Remote Viewing

Out-of-Body Experiences (OBEs) and Remote Viewing suggest that consciousness is not confined to the physical body and can exist independently. These experiences point to the possibility of a state of existence after death.

Both OBEs and Remote Viewing demonstrate **non-local consciousness**, where the mind perceives and interacts with environments beyond the physical body. This supports the idea that consciousness may continue to exist in some form after physical death, potentially in a non-physical realm where it can explore and interact without the limitations of the body.

Moreover, individuals who have experienced OBEs often describe **traveling to other realms or dimensions**. These realms are frequently depicted as beautiful, peaceful, and full of light, aligning with the descriptions from NDEs. This consistency across different experiences reinforces the idea of a non-physical afterlife where consciousness can explore new dimensions of existence.

Deathbed Visions and Shared Death Experiences

Deathbed visions and shared death experiences provide further evidence that consciousness persists after death, suggesting a transitional phase as the soul prepares to leave the body.

As individuals approach death, many report seeing **deceased loved ones** who appear to guide them through the dying process. This indicates that the afterlife may involve reunions with those who have passed before us, offering comfort and guidance during the transition from physical life to whatever lies beyond.

Shared death experiences, where those present at the moment of death perceive or feel the transition of the dying person's consciousness, suggest that the departure of the soul from the body is not a solitary experience. Instead, it can be perceived and even shared by others, further supporting the idea that consciousness continues beyond death.

A Dynamic and Continuous Afterlife

Rather than viewing the afterlife as a final destination, this new vision suggests it is a continuation of the soul's journey—a process focused on growth, reflection, and learning.

The **life review** commonly reported in NDEs implies that the afterlife involves a deep examination of one's life. This examination is not a judgment passed by an external deity but rather an opportunity for self-assessment and growth. It may help the soul understand the lessons learned during its lifetime and prepare for future experiences.

Encounters with **spiritual guides** or beings of light indicate that the afterlife is not a solitary experience. These guides offer support and wisdom, helping souls navigate the afterlife as they continue their journey of growth and understanding.

Reincarnation: A Cycle of Learning and Growth

The concept of reincarnation aligns with the idea of the afterlife as a continuous process of learning and growth. Reincarnation suggests that the soul may return to the physical world in a new body to learn new lessons or address unresolved issues from previous lives. This cycle of death and rebirth indicates that the afterlife is not an endpoint but part of an ongoing process of spiritual evolution.

Experiences like NDEs, OBEs, and deathbed visions may be part of the soul's preparation for reincarnation. These experiences offer insights and reflections that inform the soul's next incarnation, supporting the idea that the afterlife is an integral part of the soul's growth.

The Afterlife as a Non-Physical Realm

The afterlife, as suggested by these phenomena, likely exists as a non-physical realm where consciousness operates without the constraints of the physical body. OBEs and Remote Viewing suggest that the afterlife may involve different **dimensions or realms** beyond our physical understanding. These realms are often described as more vibrant, peaceful, and full of light, consistent with the descriptions provided by those who have had NDEs.

Moreover, in the afterlife, **time and space** may not function as they do in the physical world. This could explain the instantaneous travel and timeless experiences reported in OBEs and NDEs, suggesting that the afterlife is a place where the soul can exist and interact in ways that are not bound by physical limitations.

Toward a New Theory of the Afterlife

Based on the evidence from these paranormal phenomena, we can propose a new theory of the afterlife that incorporates several key ideas:

First, **consciousness is fundamental** to existence. It is not merely a byproduct of the brain but an essential aspect of reality that continues beyond physical death. The afterlife is a realm where consciousness exists independently of the physical body, capable of growth, learning, and interaction with other conscious beings.

Second, the afterlife is a **dynamic process** rather than a static place of reward or punishment. It involves reflection, learning, and preparation for future experiences. This process may include life reviews, encounters with spiritual guides, and the possibility of reincarnation.

Third, the afterlife is **integrated with physical life**. The experiences we have in the afterlife influence our physical lives and vice versa, creating a continuous cycle of growth and evolution.

Finally, the afterlife is part of a broader **cosmology** that includes multiple dimensions or realms where consciousness can exist and interact. These realms are not governed by the same physical laws as the material world, allowing for experiences that transcend our current understanding of reality.

Rethinking Reality and the Purpose of Life

Exploring the idea that consciousness survives death forces us to rethink fundamental aspects of reality, the purpose of life, and the ethical choices we make daily.

If consciousness continues beyond the physical body, it challenges the materialistic view that the physical universe is the only reality. Instead, consciousness might be the foundation of reality, with the physical world being one layer of a more complex, multi-dimensional existence.

This broader understanding of reality implies that life and death are interconnected aspects of a continuous journey. Death is not an end but a transition from one state of existence to another. This perspective reframes our understanding of life as part of a larger, ongoing process of growth and evolution.

Living with Purpose and Mindfulness

Understanding that consciousness may continue beyond death can inspire us to live with greater purpose and mindfulness. If life is part of a larger journey, it becomes essential to focus on experiences that contribute to personal growth, fulfillment, and the well-being of others. This might mean prioritizing relationships, pursuing passions, and engaging in activities that align with our values.

Furthermore, the idea of an afterlife encourages us to live with **compassion and ethical responsibility**. Knowing that our actions may have lasting consequences beyond this life can foster greater empathy and a commitment to treating others with kindness.

Exploring the Complexities of the Afterlife

While much of the evidence for the afterlife suggests peace and growth, there are also more complex and speculative aspects to consider. For instance, some theories propose the existence of **lost or wandering souls**—spirits who do not transition smoothly into the afterlife. These earthbound spirits might remain attached to the physical world due to unresolved emotions, sudden or traumatic deaths, or strong attachments to their previous lives.

Another speculative idea is that the afterlife might consist of **multiple layers or dimensions**. Some traditions suggest that souls may reside in lower astral planes if they are not yet ready to move on to higher levels. These planes could be places where souls confront unresolved issues or negative emotions, adding complexity to the notion of the afterlife.

Finally, there is the possibility that the afterlife involves **challenges or obstacles** that souls must navigate. Some reports suggest the existence of malevolent entities within the afterlife that might influence or challenge souls on their journey. Although these ideas are more speculative and less supported by empirical evidence, they raise intriguing questions about the full nature of the afterlife.

Embracing the Mystery of the Afterlife

As we explore the afterlife, it is crucial to acknowledge the limits of our current understanding. While much of the evidence points to a continuation of consciousness after death, the specifics of what this entails remain largely unknown and open to interpretation. Speculative ideas like lost souls, layered dimensions, and challenges within the afterlife encourage us to think creatively about what might await us after death.

Speculation, while not as well-supported by empirical evidence, can still offer value in broadening our perspectives. It allows us to consider the full range of possibilities regarding the afterlife and encourages further investigation into areas that are not yet fully understood.

A Call for a Broader Scientific Approach

The reluctance of mainstream science to engage with these phenomena is understandable given the emphasis on repeatability, objectivity, and empirical verification. However, when it comes to the mysteries of consciousness, the afterlife, and other paranormal occurrences, the traditional scientific method reaches its limits. These phenomena cannot always be easily reproduced or quantified, but they still demand serious investigation.

For science to progress toward a more complete understanding of the universe, it must be willing to expand its boundaries and include these unexplained phenomena within its scope of study. This does not mean abandoning scientific rigor but adapting it to explore areas that have been traditionally neglected or deemed too controversial.

The Necessity of Open-Mindedness

As we move forward, it is crucial for both scientists and the public to approach these topics with open-mindedness and a willingness to entertain possibilities that may initially seem implausible. The history of science is full of examples of once-fringe ideas that were later validated and became foundational to our understanding of the world.

The phenomena discussed in this book—whether it be the persistence of consciousness after death, the existence of non-physical entities, or the ability to access information beyond the normal sensory channels—demand a rethinking of the conventional boundaries between science and the paranormal. Only by embracing a broader perspective can we hope to develop a more complete theory of the universe, one that accounts for all aspects of human experience, including those that remain shrouded in mystery.

CONCLUSION: A CALL TO EXPLORE THE UNKNOWN

In conclusion, I urge the scientific community, scholars, and readers alike to consider these phenomena not as anomalies to be dismissed but as vital clues in the puzzle of existence. The time has come to bridge the gap between science and the unexplained, to foster a deeper exploration of the unknown, and to develop theories that encompass the full spectrum of human experience.

By doing so, we not only advance our understanding of the universe but also honor the richness and complexity of the world we inhabit—a world where the line between the known and the unknown is far less defined than we might have previously thought. In this spirit of curiosity and open inquiry, we may one day arrive at a more profound understanding of our place in the cosmos and the true nature of reality itself.

THE CONVERGENCE OF EVIDENCE

Throughout our journey, we've explored a spectrum of phenomena that challenge conventional understandings of consciousness and reality. Each topic—whether near-death experiences, reincarnation, or encounters with mediums—adds a piece to a puzzle that seems to be pointing in a singular, intriguing direction.

Take near-death experiences (NDEs), for instance. Even if one is skeptical about ghosts or the paranormal, the consistency and depth of NDE accounts present a compelling case worth considering. Individuals from diverse cultures and backgrounds report remarkably similar experiences: sensations of detachment from the body, traversing through tunnels toward light, and profound feelings of peace. Some even recount verifiable details from their surroundings while they were clinically unresponsive—details they could not have known through conventional means. These accounts pose challenging questions that modern science has yet to fully address.

If doubts persist regarding mediums or out-of-body experiences, the documented cases of reincarnation offer further food for thought. Young children, often between the ages of two and five, have provided detailed memories of past lives—including names, locations, and events—that have been later verified through historical records. These instances are difficult to explain within the current scientific framework, which struggles to account for how such precise information could be obtained without direct experience.

The narratives we've discussed are not just isolated anecdotes; they represent a vast collection of experiences reported across different times and cultures. In fact, what we've covered so far is merely the snowflake atop an immense iceberg of evidence. The convergence of these accounts from various disciplines makes them increasingly hard to dismiss. The statistical improbability of numerous independent stories all pointing toward the same possibility suggests that there may be underlying truths worth exploring.

Yet, despite the accumulating evidence, mainstream science often overlooks or minimizes these phenomena, perhaps because they don't fit neatly within established theories. This brings us to an intriguing intersection with one of the most advanced and enigmatic fields of study: quantum physics.

Quantum physics, the foundation of many modern technological advancements over the past century, deals with the behavior of particles at the smallest scales. It's a realm where the rules of classical physics no longer apply, and where particles can exist in multiple states simultaneously—a concept known as superposition. Upon observation or measurement, these particles 'collapse' into a single state, a phenomenon that has puzzled scientists for decades.

This leads us to a profound question that quantum physicists grapple with: What causes the collapse of the wave function? Is it merely the act of measurement, or does the consciousness of the observer play a crucial role? Some interpretations of quantum mechanics suggest that consciousness might indeed influence this process, implying that the observer is not just a passive participant but an active contributor to the unfolding of physical reality.

If consciousness does have a role in shaping the fundamental aspects of the physical world, this could offer a new perspective on the phenomena we've been discussing. It might help explain why certain experiences—currently unexplained by traditional science—occur with such consistency across different individuals and cultures.

While this area of inquiry remains speculative and is the subject of ongoing debate within the scientific community, it highlights the potential interconnectedness between consciousness and the fabric of the universe. It invites us to consider that our understanding of reality may be incomplete without a deeper exploration of consciousness itself.

As we continue to examine the convergence of evidence from various fields—ranging from personal accounts and psychological studies to cutting-edge physics—we are encouraged to keep an open mind. The statistical unlikelihood of all these independent lines of evidence aligning by mere chance is significant. Perhaps, by integrating insights from these diverse disciplines, we can move closer to uncovering answers to some of the most profound questions about existence.

In the following chapters, we'll delve deeper into how these ideas from quantum physics intersect with our exploration of consciousness. By doing so, we aim to shed light on the possibilities that lie at the frontier of science and human understanding, acknowledging the mysteries that compel us to look beyond the known and consider the vast potential of what might be.

CONSCIOUSNESS AND THE QUANTUM ENIGMA

Throughout this journey, we've examined a wide range of phenomena—near-death experiences, reincarnation, out-of-body experiences, and apparitions. While these may seem to be isolated stories from different fields, they all converge on one point: consciousness. At each step, consciousness seems to play a pivotal role in shaping and interacting with reality. But perhaps the most compelling case for the importance of consciousness doesn't just come from these paranormal experiences—it comes from the heart of one of the most cutting-edge and mysterious fields of science: **quantum physics**.

Quantum mechanics, the branch of science that governs the behavior of particles at the smallest scales, is responsible for nearly all of the technological advancements of the last century. It has given us lasers, computers, medical imaging, and more. Yet despite its massive impact, quantum mechanics harbors mysteries that challenge our very understanding of reality—and at the center of those mysteries is the role of **consciousness**.

THE DOUBLE-SLIT EXPERIMENT

One of the most famous experiments in quantum mechanics is the **double-slit experiment**. In its simplest form, the experiment involves firing particles, such as electrons, at a barrier with two slits. Behind the barrier is a detector, which records where each particle lands.

When the particles pass through the slits without being observed, they behave like waves, creating an interference pattern on the detector. This pattern suggests that each particle doesn't choose one slit or the other; instead, it acts as if it passes through both slits at once—existing in a state of probability, or **superposition**. But when we observe the particles—when we measure which slit they pass through—something remarkable happens. The wave-like behavior collapses, and the particles behave like solid objects, passing through only one slit and landing in distinct places on the detector.

This phenomenon, known as the **collapse of the wave function**, raises a profound question: What causes the collapse? Is it the physical measurement, or could the act of **conscious observation** itself be responsible?

THE MEASUREMENT PROBLEM

The **measurement problem** in quantum mechanics is one of the most perplexing issues in science. In quantum theory, particles exist in a state of potential, where they can occupy many possible positions or states at once. It's only when a measurement is made—when the system is observed—that these probabilities collapse into one definite state.

But what constitutes a "measurement"? In the classical view, it's simply the interaction between a particle and a measuring device that causes the collapse. However, some interpretations of quantum mechanics—most notably the **von Neumann-Wigner interpretation**—suggest that **consciousness** itself may be required to collapse the wave function. In this view, the universe exists in a state of potential until it is observed by a conscious being, at which point reality "snaps" into a definite state.

This idea is uncomfortable for many physicists, and understandably so. If consciousness is required to bring reality into existence, it challenges the very foundation of materialism—the belief that the physical world exists independently of our perceptions. It suggests that **consciousness is not a passive observer** of the universe but an active participant in shaping it.

Because of these implications, alternative interpretations of quantum mechanics have been developed to avoid involving consciousness. Some, like the **Many Worlds interpretation**, propose that the wave function never collapses at all. Instead, each possible outcome of a quantum event creates a new, parallel universe, so all possibilities are realized in different realities. Others, like **decoherence theory**, explain the collapse in terms of interactions between particles and their environments, without the need for an observer.

Yet despite these interpretations, the idea that consciousness plays a role in the collapse of the wave function remains a compelling one. It may not be the only explanation, but it is a simple and intuitive one—Occam's Razor suggests that the simplest explanation is often the best, and in this case, the simplest explanation may be that **conscious observation collapses the wave function**.

DELAYED-CHOICE EXPERIMENTS

As scientists probed deeper into quantum mechanics, experiments like John Wheeler's **delayed-choice experiment** pushed the boundaries of our understanding even further. In this variation of the double-slit experiment, the decision of whether or not to observe the particle is made after the particle has already passed through the slits. Incredibly, even when the choice to observe the particle is made after the fact, the particle still "chooses" to behave either as a wave or a particle, depending on whether or not it is measured.

It's as if the particle "knows" whether it will be observed, even after it has already passed through the slits, and adjusts its behavior accordingly. This suggests that the act of observation—or more intriguingly, **conscious observation**—not only affects the present but may also influence events that have already happened.

The implications of the delayed-choice experiment are mind-boggling. If consciousness plays a role in collapsing the wave function, it might not only influence the present but also **shape the past**. This retroactive influence defies our intuitive understanding of time and causality, raising profound questions about the nature of reality itself.

THE IMPORTANCE OF CONSCIOUSNESS IN SHAPING REALITY

The connection between quantum mechanics and consciousness is not just a theoretical puzzle—it suggests a deeper truth about the nature of reality. In the quantum world, particles exist in a state of potential until they are observed. This is not just a quirk of particles at the smallest scales; it may be a fundamental feature of reality itself.

If consciousness is required to collapse the wave function, then reality, as we experience it, is not something that exists independently of us. Instead, reality may be **observer-**

dependent—brought into being by the conscious mind. This idea resonates with the philosophical concept of **idealism**, which holds that reality is fundamentally mental rather than material. In this view, consciousness is the foundation of existence, and the physical world emerges from consciousness, not the other way around.

This perspective also aligns with many of the paranormal phenomena we've explored throughout this book. Near-death experiences, reincarnation, and out-of-body experiences all suggest that consciousness is not confined to the brain but may exist independently of the body. If consciousness is fundamental to reality, it stands to reason that it could persist beyond death, interact with the physical world in ways we don't fully understand, and even transcend time.

OCCAM'S RAZOR

When faced with multiple competing explanations, Occam's Razor advises us to choose the one that requires the fewest assumptions. The alternative interpretations of quantum mechanics—such as the Many Worlds Theory—are complex and introduce a vast array of assumptions, such as the existence of countless parallel universes. In contrast, the idea that consciousness collapses the wave function is relatively simple. It requires us to accept only that consciousness plays a fundamental role in shaping reality—a concept already suggested by the convergence of evidence from various disciplines.

By applying Occam's Razor, we can see that the consciousness-based interpretation of quantum mechanics provides a straightforward and intuitive explanation for the collapse of the wave function. It also ties into the broader theme we've explored throughout this book: that **consciousness is the key** to understanding the mysteries of life, death, and the nature of existence.

CONSCIOUSNESS AS THE FOUNDATION OF REALITY

The evidence we've explored—from near-death experiences and reincarnation to quantum mechanics—points us in a remarkable direction. Consciousness appears to be more than just a product of the brain; it may be the very force that shapes reality. If consciousness is required to collapse the wave function, then the universe as we know it exists in a state of potential until it is observed by a conscious mind.

This realization opens up a world of possibilities. It suggests that reality is not fixed and independent but fluid and observer-dependent. It hints that consciousness may not only persist after death but also influence the physical world in ways we are only beginning to understand.

As we conclude this exploration, one thing becomes clear: consciousness is not just a passive observer of the universe but an **active creator**. Whether through quantum mechanics or paranormal phenomena, the evidence suggests that **consciousness is the foundation of reality itself**. And if that is true, then our understanding of life, death, and the universe is poised for a revolution.

BEYOND THE HORIZON OF THE KNOWN

As we come to the end of this journey, it becomes clear that the boundaries of what we know are not as solid as we once believed. From the everyday mysteries of life and death to the profound questions posed by quantum physics, the evidence points to one undeniable conclusion: consciousness is not a mere byproduct of the brain, nor is it something easily explained by materialism. It may very well be the cornerstone of reality itself.

Throughout these pages, we've explored a variety of phenomena—near-death experiences, reincarnation, out-of-body experiences, and the eerie echoes of past lives. These accounts, while often dismissed as mere anecdote or superstition, hold within them patterns that can no longer be ignored. They converge on the idea that **consciousness transcends the physical**. And as we've seen, this convergence extends beyond personal stories and ancient traditions—it reaches deep into the heart of modern science.

Quantum physics, the very foundation of our technological age, has revealed that the universe operates on principles far stranger than we ever imagined. The simple act of observation can collapse waves of probability into the hard, concrete world we experience. Consciousness, it seems, may be woven into the fabric of the universe in ways we are only beginning to understand.

This book has not been about proving any one theory or forcing a single conclusion. Instead, it has been an exploration—an invitation to rethink the limits of what we consider possible. The **convergence of evidence** suggests that consciousness is not only vital to our personal experiences but also to the structure of reality itself. **Beyond a reasonable doubt**, we are led to the idea that consciousness may be the key to unlocking the mysteries of existence.

And yet, for all that we have uncovered, there is still so much we don't know. The true nature of consciousness remains one of the greatest enigmas, lying just beyond the horizon of our understanding. But now, with the evidence laid before us, the question is no longer whether we can afford to explore it, but how we can afford not to.

Science and spirituality, long thought to be incompatible, are slowly beginning to overlap. As the evidence converges from different disciplines—quantum physics, neuroscience, psychology, and the testimonies of those who have touched the other side—we are being called to reexamine our understanding of reality. This is not about replacing science with belief, but about broadening our methods of inquiry. Perhaps the tools we need to answer the big questions are ones we have not yet fully developed.

What lies ahead is a frontier. A new way of thinking about the universe, one where **consciousness is at the center** rather than on the periphery. This frontier isn't just for scientists or philosophers. It's a journey for each of us to explore, not only with our minds but with our experiences, our openness to the unknown, and our willingness to question the old models that no longer serve us.

The afterlife, reincarnation, and consciousness may not be phenomena that fit neatly into the boxes of traditional science, but that does not mean they are unworthy of serious exploration. The convergence of evidence shows us that these are not isolated mysteries, but interconnected pieces of a larger puzzle—one that reveals a deeper truth about our existence.

We may never fully understand consciousness, but every step forward brings us closer to the answers we seek. And along the way, we find not just answers but new questions, new paths, and new horizons. Perhaps this is the true nature of consciousness: not a destination, but an endless journey, one that expands as we evolve in our understanding.

As we move beyond the horizon of what we know, we enter a new era of exploration. An era where consciousness, rather than being an afterthought, becomes the guiding force in understanding not just the universe, but ourselves. And in that exploration, we just might find that the greatest mysteries are not out there, but within us.

For more books by Jamie visit

www.areghostsreal.info

If you enjoyed the book and found it thought-provoking, I would greatly appreciate it if you could leave a review. Your feedback not only helps other readers discover the book but also encourages further exploration into the fascinating world of the paranormal. Your support means a lot!

Made in the USA
Middletown, DE
29 May 2025